The Secrets of
SUCCESSFUL
LEADERSHIP AND
PEOPLE MANAGEMENT

About the author

Born in Edgware, Middlesex, longer ago than he dares think about, **Clive Goodworth** was for twenty years a regular officer in the Royal Air Force. In 1968 he joined the Road Transport Industry Training Board as a training adviser where he spent two years before becoming a senior personnel executive with an international oil company. In 1975 he went into teaching and became Senior Lecturer in Management and Professional Studies at the Huntingdonshire College. A few years ago he decided to devote himself to full-time writing.

Books in the series

The Secrets of Successful Business Letters   Clive Goodworth

The Secrets of Successful Copywriting   Patrick Quinn

The Secrets of Successful Direct Response Marketing Frank Jefkins

The Secrets of Successful Hiring and Firing   Clive Goodworth

The Secrets of Successful Low-budget Advertising Patrick Quinn

The Secrets of Successful Low-budget Exhibitions John Powell and Patrick Quinn

The Secrets of Successful PR and Image-making Tony Greener

The Secrets of Successful Sales Management   Tony Adams

The Secrets of Successful Selling   Tony Adams

The Secrets of Successful Speaking and Business Presentations   Gordon Bell

The Secrets of Successful Telephone Selling   Chris de Winter

The Secrets of
SUCCESSFUL LEADERSHIP AND PEOPLE MANAGEMENT

Clive Goodworth

HEINEMANN PROFESSIONAL PUBLISHING

Heinemann Professional Publishing Ltd
Halley Court, Jordan Hill, Oxford OX2 8EJ

OXFORD   LONDON   MELBOURNE   AUCKLAND   SINGAPORE
IBADAN   NAIROBI   GABORONE   KINGSTON

First published 1988
First published as a paperback edition 1990

British Library Cataloguing in Publication Data

Goodworth, Clive T.
The Secrets of successful leadership
and people management
1. Management. Leadership. Assessment
I. Title
658.4'092

ISBN 0 434 90691 2

Photoset by Deltatype Ltd, Ellesmere Port
Printed in Great Britain by
Billings of Worcester Ltd

AN ESSENTIAL PREAMBLE

When it comes to the Sex Discrimination Act, *et al*, and the business of using pronouns, I – like many of my pen-pushing brethren – have something of a problem. Like it or not, there are times when the inclusion of such non-sexist bits as 'his or her' make for really heavy reading and, for the sake of simplicity, in this book I've reduced them to a minimum. If any reader is offended by this deliberate economy, I apologise.

Contents

1 So just get out there and manage   1

As a scene-setter, a management horror story
– something on how managers are made –
management styles: the autocrat; the laissez
faire merchant; the paternalistic manager; the
democrat; the management fraud; the
consultative-cum-participative manager.
Workbox Number 1 (for the super-keen!)

2 But am I really like that?   21

A management questionnaire – a spot of
candid introspection on your personality – an
analysis of the responses to the questionnaire –
drawing the strings together on aspects of
your personality.
Workbox Number 2

3 Now, what are they really like?   40

A questionnaire on your knowledge of your
subordinates – the tactical advantages of
Nosey Parker management – comments on the
questionnaire – the dreaded blacklist of bad
performers: dealing with poor performers and
offenders; recognizing odd-ball personalities –
motivating for results.
Workbox Number 3

4 It's the job that counts   59
Why job descriptions? – job analysis and job
descriptions in some detail – the employee
specification — job evaluation – the
identification of training needs – something on
planning training and training methods –
training evaluation – job enrichment – pay
systems – suggestion schemes.
Workbox Number 4

5 Garbage in – and, yes, garbage out   79
Planning delegation – some delegation
clangers –how best to get things done:
instructing; allocating; consulting – the twin
perils of underdelegation and overdelegation.
Workbox Number 5

6 Run a team, not a prison camp   94
Salutary storytime: the deadly tale of the new
broom and the fable of the ever-open door –
the secrets of moulding them into a team, and
what is bound to happen if you don't.
Workbox Number 6

Recommended reading   117

Additional response columns for Chapter 2   118

Panic index   126

1   So just get out there and manage

AN INTRODUCTION TO THE PERILS OF THE MANAGEMENT HOT SEAT

Tell you what, let's rid ourselves of the dull old textbook bit right at the outset. Consider, if you will, a dictionary definition of that much-vaunted, ill-used term, *manager*:

> **manager** One who conducts the working of, has effective control of, bends others to his or her will, cajoles, finds a way, contrives to get along, is clever or stupid enough to bring about, secures, deals with.

I find it gratifying that even the dictionary seeks to remind us of the inglorious affinity between management and stupidity – because, reader, that is what this initial chapter is all about. First, I'd like you to accompany me on a gentle romp through just one or two instances of idiocy in managing people – and then, if you're still with me, we'll plonk the lid on what is essentially a scene-setting *pot-pourri* by taking a swift glance at some chunks of management biology. And by the way, it mightn't be such a bad idea if you regard these gadabout preliminaries as a form of pre-op medication – for the simple reason that, once we've finished with them, it's not going to be me who gets strapped to the dissection slab.

Hello and welcome – we'll kick off with a story.

Once upon a time, there was a certain managing director – a truly mercurial, dyed-in-the-wool autocrat who, not surprisingly, ruled his international empire by the age-old expedient of being a do-it-my-way, one-man band. Now, this kept the MD very busy, not least because his compulsion to be everywhere at once involved him in a great deal of air travel –

which brings us to the point of our tale. It was on such high-altitude occasions when, doubtless due to his closer proximity to the Great Chairman in the Sky, he was regularly susceptible to heaven-sent, soul-shaking inspirations.

You'll probably agree that there's little wrong with having inspirations, especially the divine variety – but, in this guy's case, there was a monumental snag. Sadly, it so happened that the striving Big Daddy was totally infected with that virulent executive bug, the action-this-day syndrome. Thus it was that, all too often, Monday's airborne vision became Tuesday's company policy and, every now and again, Wednesday's company clanger.

Take the fateful time when, poised in mid-Atlantic and anxiously awaiting his next dollop of spiritual enlightenment, our hero was suddenly assailed by the mind-bending proposition that *his outfit's employees were the key to corporate success*. While it's likely that flight safety regulations precluded the appearance of a burning bush in the airliner's cabin, for all that, the celestial message was loud and clear – and, in the twinkling of an eye, the MD became privy to a full-blown, twenty-four carat revelation.

In short, he saw the promised land; an El Dorado in which his many, widely-dispersed employees surmounted the barriers of disparity and distance to become as one – a worldwide army of warriors-cum-chums, all striving together for a common goal. And, being the creature he was, he liked what he saw – particularly when his inspiration didn't end there, but went on to detail the ways and means by which he could achieve this wondrous commercial nirvana.

That, reader, is how the seeds of the MD's 'People Programme' were sown – and it was only a matter of hours before his long-suffering acolytes back at head office found themselves holding their umpteenth snarling tiger by the tail. Lightly disguised as a Chief Executive's memorandum, the bombshell plunged onto their desks and, sure as hell, swiftly enveloped them in its lethal fallout:

> I require you to take immediate steps to devise and duly
> implement a group-wide scheme to foster an overriding

sense of well-being and loyalty in all our employees. The scheme, which will be known as the People Programme, will recognize above all else that:

- Our employees are our most valuable asset.
- No matter what role an individual may play within the organization, each and every employee is a vital and respected member of our corporate family.

Heaven preserve us, his minions must have thought, here we go again. They read on – and almost certainly blanched at the gills.

Initially, the People Programme will embrace certain priority measures; namely:

1 A distinctive lapel badge is to be designed and produced forthwith. The badge will consist of a suitable corporate emblem, to be agreed by me, and each will be consecutively numbered. The number, which is to form part of the badge motif, will serve as the holder's membership number in the People Programme. In this context, I expect to receive badge Number 1.

2 Individual membership cards complete with passport-type photographs are to be produced and issued to all employees.

3 A bi-monthly, prestige house journal is to be introduced forthwith. The journal, entitled *People Matter*, will be edited by .... (*what a thrill it must have been for this lucky person*) and I require detailed proposals for the first issue by the end of this month.

4 A copy of the forthcoming Annual Report and Accounts is to be supplied to each employee, together with an introductory letter which I shall be preparing.

You will appreciate that the successful implementation of this first phase of the People Programme will do much to enhance individual and corporate morale (*blah, blah, blah and more blah*).

Metaphorically speaking, the immediate result of this edict was that the head office corridors echoed with silent screams as the hapless managers bemoaned their fate and, of course, engaged in their usual litany of cursing the MD, the Wright brothers and all the other pioneers of air travel. Despite their common agreement that the MD had finally taken leave of his marbles, no one was left in any doubt that his devilish new baby was squatting firmly on, and thoroughly wetting, their respective laps.

Little is known of the frenetic activity that followed but one thing is for sure, money was spent like water. The head office was inundated with badge purveyors, printers' reps, designers and the like – all of them drawn by that powerful magnet, the scent of an easy buck. Meeting after meeting was held, with the MD presiding over each one and, true to form, stomping with the delicacy of a charging rhino on this and that cautious conclusion. No, a veil is drawn over this part of our story so, without further ado, let's move on to what actually happened when the so-called People Programme was launched on the unsuspecting heads of the employees concerned.

But, first, call to mind the likely outcome when a buccaneering autocrat of a boss has the proverbial bit held firmly between his teeth. Put it this way, despite the fact that our MD banned such terms as 'conglomerate' and 'asset-stripping' from his outfit's vocabulary, all types of new acquisitions appeared and disappeared with monotonous regularity. So it shouldn't come as a surprise that many of the surviving employees regarded their particular ivory tower with healthy suspicion. This, then, was the climate in which all and sundry were suddenly invited – no, commanded – to become a united and happy family.

On the appointed day, parcels of tinkling metalware were despatched post-haste to all points of the corporate compass – blue badges for the shipping employees, red badges for the insurance wallahs, yellow for those in manufacturing and so on. What happened then, do you ask? Well, the zero-hour scene at Big Daddy's headquarters provides an apt analogy of the goings-on in the rest of his empire. While many of the pen-pushers greeted the things with dire suspicion and a deal of earthy comment, nearly all of them decided that discretion was the better part of valour – with the result that lapels positively twinkled with the gilded adornments. True, one junior accountant (who knew he was for the chop, anyway), was defiant enough to wear his badge upside down – and it was interesting to witness how certain senior managers strolled around with slightly self-conscious mien, eyeing each other surreptitiously to see if anyone had ignored the edict.

However, within a short time, the concept that the working masses would approve of regulational badge-bearing plonked to the floor like a lump of wet dough and, with the notable exception of a few who probably wore them in bed, nearly two thousand of the expensive, multi-coloured trinkets passed into limbo.

Which brings us to the issue of the membership cards – with individual photographs, you'll recall. Well, this feature of the People Programme took several weeks to achieve, mainly because a head office fall-guy was required to lug his hefty camera-cum-laminator plus a crateful of gubbins all over the place, taking mug-shots wherever he went. My, how that poor chap must have suffered. There was but one common reaction to his efforts, 'What in hell are these for?' The much-publicized exhortation that the cards would form an intrinsic part of a forthcoming discount purchase scheme fell on deaf ears. 'First, it's badges, now it's identity cards – when do we get our rifles?' became the cry of the day.

If, thus far, it seems to you that the MD's divinely-inspired plan was going somewhat awry – why, you're dead right. However, bide with me, for now we come to the crunch, our visionary big-wig's *pièce de résistance* – his prestige house journal, *People Matter*.

Funnily enough, it appears that many of the head office staff rallied to this particular cause – and, by dint of much head-scratching, a very creditable proof emerged from the chaos. It's important to note that the conscripted editor was quite confident that his inaugural issue of *People Matter* reflected a nice degree of 'democratic expression' – and that it wouldn't be rejected out of hand by the widespread and diverse readership as purely a medium for company propaganda. So, if we are to believe history, on the dot of the appointed hour the proof copy was trotted into the MD's sanctum to receive his stamp of approval. And, minutes later, all hell broke loose. 'What in blazes do you think you're up to?' roared the boss, his face a delicate shade of puce. 'This is a finished proof and I haven't even had a chance to vet the copy!'

The message was stark and simple. Democratic expression was strictly for the birds – *People Matter* was destined to be *the MD's* journal, with every article, word and picture subject to the arrant blue pencil of Big Daddy, himself. Disillusioned and unhappy, the editorial team crept back to their hidey-hole where, as instructed, they proceeded to prostitute their newly-acquired art. Eventually, the thing was published and earned the lukewarm, ironic reception that it undoubtedly deserved. As for being a 'prestige journal' – well, you've got to be joking.

Finally, we come to the provision of a copy of the annual report and accounts to every Jack and Jill employee of this polyglot organization. In course of time, each subsidiary company at home and abroad duly received its heavy bale of glossies for distribution; but, unfortunately, there was a hiccup, in that barely any of the employees were in the mood to appreciate this further token of mandatory goodwill. Within hours, company loos over three continents were strewn with the immensely expensive freebies which, you understand, had been printed on such superb, heavyweight paper that it was virtually impossible to flush them away. The feedback from the subsidiaries took the form of an ominous and concerted rumble – to the effect that, if money was so freely available, the gooks at head office would do well to forget their grandiose ideas and simply put it in the pay packets.

There's not much left to tell. The mind-blinkered, auto-cratic head of this organization knew full well what people thought of his much-vaunted People Programme but that didn't matter. Armed with his divine inspirations and a bevy of subservient underlings, he went on to perpetrate bigger and better blunders – for he was the boss and *he knew what was good for them.*

Well that's the end of the ice-breaking story. If you ask me why on earth I decided to kick off in such fashion, I haven't the faintest notion – except to mention that, if we're going to take a look at successful leadership and people management, it isn't such a bad idea to remind ourselves of the baddies of the executive world.

And, lest we harbour any illusions, that includes you and me.

I'M A MANAGER BECAUSE THAT'S WHAT I'M CALLED

How did you first become a manager?

Was it the case that, having shone as an operative, a clerk, a shop assistant or whatever, a perceptive boss saw in you the potential for promotion and, forthwith, put you through carefully designed and protracted training in management – with the twofold aim of really assessing your worth and, if all went well, arming you for the fray?

Or, just perhaps, were you elevated to a management hot seat in much the same way that I, and umpteen like me, gained those executive spurs? Take, for example and because you've precious little choice, what happened to Bill Horrocks.

It had all started when dear old Percy Threadgold, national sales manager at Mephitic Suppositories Ltd and doyen of the management team, was discovered by a hysterical tea lady 'all slumped and 'orrible' at his desk – cruelly despatched by way of a mercifully swift coronary. Percy's directors were thrown into testy confusion by this sudden inconvenience and, once the obsequies were over, wasted no time in holding an emergency get-together.

'Well, I don't know,' growled the MD, absent-mindedly fingering their latest product ('Britain's leading suppository – a miracle blend of whortleberry and ipecacuanha in a coal tar base'). 'We'd better go ahead and advertise the damned post.'

'No, wait a minute,' said Blenkinsop, the financial director. 'I've got a splendid idea.'

'All right, we're listening.'

'It's really quite simple,' Blenkinsop continued, his scrawny face suffused with enthusiasm. 'Why not promote Bill Horrocks? He's been with us for over seven years and, well, he knows the business inside out – quite the best salesman we've ever had.'

Hmmm, Blenkinsop's right, thought the MD, Horrocks is almost certainly the man – seven years' service, excellent performance, knows the products like the back of his hand.

'Yes, that's exactly what I had in mind,' he said flatly. 'Right – all in favour of Horrocks getting the job . . .'

As usual, there were no dissenters and in no time Bill was plucked from his base in the West Country to fill the still-warm seat at head office. He could hardly credit his good luck and, being a man of considerable determination, set to with a will to make a resounding success of his new appointment. He'd arrived and, by George, he'd show them.

His first gambit was to convene a meeting of the sales force – when, encouraged by what he interpreted as an attentive and supportive silence, Bill spoke at length on exactly how he planned to tackle his new responsibilities. It was only when the meeting broke up that things went terribly wrong. To his utter dismay, three of the team handed in their resignations, declaring angrily that they were not prepared to work for a 'jumped-up little dictator who didn't know his knee from his elbow'.

This was serious enough, but over the next four weeks Bill's fortunes went from bad to worse. Scrabbling frantically and ineffectively to make a success of his now hated job, he made a complete pig's ear of the sales returns, alienated three major customers with ill-composed and totally unjustified letters and generally created mayhem in the previously happy and well-organized department.

And, of course, the inevitable happened. Galvanized into furious action, the MD fired a quick bullet from the hip and despatched poor Bill on the rocky road to the dole queue. Then, since honour had yet to be satisfied, the MD followed tradition to the letter and turned on the vainly protesting Blenkinsop.

'It's all down to you – if I hadn't listened to your silly suggestion, none of this would've happened.'

And so on, ad infinitum.

Now, let's get one thing straight. In asking whether you, reader, were promoted to your first management slot in much the same way as poor old Bill, I'm *not* implying that you went on to make a complete mess of things – goodness, perish the thought! No, I just wish to establish whether your meteoric ascent to management was in general accordance with what we can call, for want of a better term, the Great British Promotion Panjandrum.★

The GBPP is, of course, an allusion to the age-old method by which the vast majority of promotions are carried out. You know it and I know it. Despite the worries and heartache endured by myriad promotees and, even more important, despite the sufferings of the hapless souls who have the misfortune to be under them, despite that most ominous of caveats, the Peter Principle,† we continue to create managers by intoning that stinking malediction:

You're a manager now, so just get out there – and manage.

When you think about it (and you should), it's downright criminal. Given the advent of a new process or piece of equipment, the average employer will send those who'll be concerned with whatever it is on a suitable training course, usually with the speed of light. But, and here's the tragedy, when that self-same average employer decides to promote some hapless soul to a supervisory or management post, what usually happens? Nothing, my friend, sweet nothing. Once the decision is taken, it's as if the poor sucker receives an immediate, heaven-sent injection of management know-how – and, yes, we're back to the litany, 'Congratulations, you're a manager now, so just get out there and manage.'

★At the risk of teaching you to suck eggs, during the Second World War the boffins came up with an enormous, rocket-propelled, wheel-like contraption which was intended to be set loose on the D-Day beaches with, would you believe, the object of trundling over and exploding the enemy minefields. Well, on trials (which were duly filmed, thus providing one of the funniest clips to emerge from that horrific conflict), the flame-spitting monster simply ran amok – creating an absolute bedlam of confusion, panic and strife. Hence my choice of the term, Great British Promotion Panjandrum.
†'In a hierarchy every employee tends to rise to his level of incompetence' – immortal words coined by Dr Lawrence J. Peter and Raymond Hull (*The Peter Principle – Why Things Go Wrong*, William Morrow & Company Inc., New York, 1969).

True, our training horizons are dotted with some shining examples of how potential managers should be developed and trained for the future. But, if one has the temerity to mention to the run-of-the-mill employer that his promotees would benefit from even a smidgen of, say, the Marks and Spencer philosophy – goodness, the terrible agony of it all:

Who the devil do you think I am? It's all very well for these big companies with money coming out of their ears but I've a struggle to make ends meet, as it is. I just can't afford to indulge in such luxuries and if you had any sense, you'd realize it.'

To which cry from the heart there's only one answer; the misguided ass can't afford not to – but, of course, in his myopic view, the undoubted advantages of such training aren't clearly identifiable on that vital bottom line, are they?

Having stuck with me thus far, it should be apparent to you that this scene-setting, introductory chapter is tending to wallow in gloom and doom. I make absolutely no apology for this, for we need reminding, again and again, that continuing to ignore our management hangovers from the Industrial Revolution constitutes nothing less than a recipe for personal and corporate disaster.

Let's wallow some more.

WHAT D'YOU MEAN, WHAT TYPE OF MANAGER AM I?

Okay, forget for a few minutes how you actually became a manager and think about one outstanding fact of executive life; namely, whether you like it or not (and if you could stand outside yourself, the odds are you wouldn't), every tittle of your working performance is stamped with 'your' management personality – or, if you like the more innocuous-sounding ring to it, your management style.

No, I'm sorry, but that's no good. Don't just read the words; *get off your mental butt and really think of the implications behind them*. You cannot see yourself as others see you and it's what others see (and, remember, suffer) that really counts.

Which must pose the sixty-four thousand dollar question, *what* do they see and suffer?

If you're brave enough to plough through Chapter 2, you'll probably be well on the way to facing the answer but, in the meantime, let's lead gently up to crunch-time by taking a look at what the egg-heads term the 'classic' management styles. At this stage, I wouldn't recommend any attempts at soul-searching – unless, of course, you have a burning desire to condemn yourself without benefit of trial.

We'll start with a pretty safe generalization. You can bet your boots that any manager's approach to his job and the people under him is heavily peppered with one of no more than six, widely varying management styles. Hey, what's that?

> I'll not have it, Goodworth – you just can't categorize my wonderfully complicated working personality under one of six headings, whatever they may be. Damn it man, I'm a human being, not a flaming machine.

Here, I did say 'heavily peppered', not smothered – although I venture to add that you and I can call to mind quite a few management acquaintances who *can* be precisely categorized as follows:

The autocrat

You'll recall that our opening story pictured one such personality. However, it behoves us to take a closer look at the beast's make-up, so let's do exactly that.

In the autocrat we have the boss who, gripped with an innate compulsion to dominate others to the full, takes maximum advantage of his status and power to achieve that singular objective. There's no doubt that unilateralism is his creed – and that he gets what he wants by the simple expedient of plonking his size eleven boots on size seven necks. It could also be said that he seldom regards his minions as people, but, rather, as work units – or, to put it more succinctly, as £-signs.

As the professionally skilled autocrat performs the nearest thing to a rhinoceros charge up the promotion ladder, one shouldn't be too surprised to learn that he'll often be inclined to offer this very success as a complete vindication of his style which, equally often, he'll freely acknowledge. However, and sadly, there's a whole army of autocratic so-and-sos who labour under the colossal illusion that they're anything *but* autocratic:

> Who, me – autocratic? You can't be serious – I bend over backwards with my lot to ensure that everyone gets a fair crack of the whip. (*Note the Freudian slip.*) You textbook wallahs are all the same. You say that managers should wield authority – but when someone does exactly that, you condemn him for being autocratic. Tell you what, for once, why don't *you* try dealing with that lot on the shop floor? You'd soon learn that if a manager's to do his job properly, he can't afford to let them grind him down. If that's being autocratic, then I'm a Dutch uncle. And, by the way, since you appear to have forgotten, it's your round.

No comment.

The laissez faire merchant
Unlike Mary Tudor, the laissez faire manager has three words engraved on his diminutive heart – *leave well alone*. Devoting every ounce of his extremely low energy to the overriding task of not making waves, this caricature of an executive is a professional in the old art of management by abdication. To put it in less emotional terms, the manager with laissez faire in his veins will ensure that the members of his group have absolute freedom to sort out their roles and tackle their work without an iota of control or participation by their nominated boss.

Just in case you're curious, there's an ancient precedent for such executive inaction – for it was way back in 1640 that Pierre Corneille paved the way for the management idlers' charter:

> '*Faites votre devoir et laissez faire aux dieux.*'
> '*Do your duty, and leave the issue to the Gods.*'

The paternalistic manager

While it's true that many small business proprietors (notably, the worthies who like to transfix us with gripping, well-nigh Dickensian accounts of how they've come up the hard way) are little less than pure-bred autocrats, it's equally true that a goodly number of them fall head-over-heels in love with the paternalistic approach. To be fair, there's a grain of an excuse for this in that anyone who struggles to get a small outfit going from scratch is apt to regard his close-knit team as his very own, hand-reared family of employees. But, excuse or not, we're eyeball-to-eyeball with a very dodgy management style – and, mark you, it's not only the small business proprietor who can catch this particular bug.

The trouble is, almost invariably, the paternalistic boss takes things to the ultimate and tends to treat his people like children. In his eyes, he's wholly responsible for their physical, mental and moral welfare – in and out of work, twenty-fours a day. Of course, this would be all fine and dandy – if, that is, he *was* employing children.

The democrat

At first glance, the term 'democratic management' may well ring a sweet-sounding bell and, in fact, there are quite a few textbooks around that label this particular style as the desirable pick of the bunch. However, think about it. The democratic leader is almost certainly unsure of himself and his relations with his subordinates – to the extent that everything, but everything, will be a matter for group discussion and decision. Hence, the democrat-beastie is more or less a rubber-stamping yes-man who, hoping like fury that his people will always come up with the right answers, relies on them to do just that.

Sadly, life is not a bowl of cherries and relatively few subordinates are sufficiently self-disciplined and good at their jobs to work under such lack-lustre management. If you'll pardon a faintly inept simile, the democratic manager is at the helm of a balsa wood boat and no one will be more surprised than the hapless skipper when the craft becomes waterlogged.

The management fraud

It matters little whether this particular denizen of the executive jungle bears an autocratic, paternalistic or what-have-you outward stamp. Whatever his skin-deep style, deep down under he's nothing but an artful, scheming conniver – hell-bent on nobbling anyone who, in his twisted view, stands in the way of his insidious ploys at self-preservation and advancement. You know him and I know him – the type who will say one thing to your face and then do the opposite; who'll skilfully blame his poor subordinates for anything under the sun rather than admit to a tittle of personal weakness; who, given the slightest inclination and the advantage of a dark night, will slip a knife between someone's ribs with consummate ease.

The consultative-cum-participative manager

And here, at long last, is the goodie in our mini-pile. This uncommon treasure is the professionally trained and experienced boss who, practising the art of consultation to the full without sacrificing a scrap of control, makes his own decisions and, what's more, stands by them. The C-cum-P manager encourages participation and delegates wisely and well but never, ever loses sight of the fact that he bears the crucial responsibility of leadership. It's hardly surprising, then, that he is inclined to favour that good old adage, 'There are no bad Indians, only bad Chiefs.'

A PAUSE FOR A BREATHER

Having duly decided that your personal style is superbly consultative-cum-participative, there seems little point in going on – unless, of course, you'd like to confirm your diagnosis. I do hope so, for the fun is about to commence.

WORKBOX NUMBER 1 (FOR THE SUPER-KEEN!)

You'll find one of these workboxes at the end of each chapter – and, yes, it's back to school with a vengeance. But take heart, the primary purpose of these mini-exercises and other bits and pieces is to provide you with food for thought, not test your knowledge – says he, lying through his teeth.

You'll need a pencil and paper – and, as always when it comes to dealing with folk and their ways, bags of imagination. By the way, don't expect to find cut-and-dried answers at the end of each workbox, will you? People management is not a '2 + 2 = 4' subject like chemistry or accounts; it's what the boffins would probably term an 'organic' topic – as with a lump of yeasty dough, one can poke it at one end and it bulges at the other. What you will find are 'trigger answers' – comments, tips and what-not which, once again, are designed to jog your brain cells into thinking about *your* people.

And the jolly best of luck!

Teaser 1
Think in terms of leadership and imagine that you're required to list *ten* personal qualities which any leader should possess. Well, go on, then – do exactly that.

Teaser 2
You'll probably agree that the quality of one's perception of people is an important factor, especially when managing them. What follows is a narrative report on a certain manager which, although she's alive and kicking, has been shrouded in anonymity. Please read it carefully.

Patricia Parkinson-Browne
Once seen, Patricia Parkinson-Browne, aged 49, unmarried, is not easily forgotten. Tall, albeit overweight for her height, she dresses immaculately and well – particularly at the office, where her overall appearance and upright bearing are the subjects of much favourable and, inevitably, some envious comment. Suffice it to say that her managing director describes Parkinson-Browne as 'eminently well-groomed for her role' as personnel manager at a successful and go-ahead engineering company.

Although Parkinson-Browne made the most of a sound grammar school education and achieved her qualifications for entrance to university, she decided against pursuing her academic studies and, instead, successfully competed for a short service commission in the secretarial branch of the Women's Royal Air Force. At the completion of her training, she was awarded the Sash of Honour for the best all-round performance of her entry – an achievement that augured well for her Service career. As with all officers of the armed forces, her subsequent progress-cum-performance was the subject of regular and detailed confidential reports by her successive commanding officers – and the following comments are excerpts, given in chronological order, from some of these reports:

- 'This young woman has displayed commendable qualities of management in every aspect of her work. Given due experience, I believe she will go far.'

- 'Very commendably, Parkinson-Browne insists on striving for personal perfection in her work. I am bound to say, however, that her utter zeal in requiring an exactly similar standard from her subordinates needs to be tempered with tolerance – a quality which she appears to lack.'

- 'Parkinson-Browne remains a perfectionist in her work, and cannot be praised too highly for the manner in which she has maintained these self-imposed and wholly rigorous standards. I must report, however, that the general morale of her section leaves something to be desired and, as a consequence, I have reminded her that an officer of her overall ability should not find it necessary to practise what I regard as an unacceptably authoritarian brand of management.'

- 'A splendid performance . . . Parkinson-Browne has succeeded in whipping a previously slack section into a near-perfect example of true Service efficiency. Immediately on her arrival at this unit, she grabbed a notoriously ineffective bunch of personnel by the ears and, brooking no excuses, knocked them into shape.'

On leaving the WRAF, Parkinson-Browne obtained a position as assistant personnel manager with her present employer. Shortly after her arrival in the post, the company experienced determined and eventually successful efforts by the Amalgamated Union of Engineering Workers (AUEW) to recruit the majority of the production workforce as members. This transformation of a previously 'non-union' company's affairs plunged Parkinson-Browne into a near-ceaseless round of meetings and negotiations with the newly-elected shop stewards and, due to the firm's enforced recognition of the AUEW, coupled with the apparent inability or unwillingness of her immediate boss to deal effectively with the union, she found herself heavily involved at the negotiation table.

It was at about this time that the company began to suffer a rapidly-shrinking order book and, as a result, Parkinson-Browne's overall attitude to the many approaches by the AUEW amply reflected the firm's determination to prune costs and limit expenditure. Her forcefulness in negotiation swiftly earned her two, diametrically-opposed reputations. On the one hand, the union regarded her as a totally coercive, unfeeling manager who cared little or nothing for the well-being of the workforce (an opinion which was heartily shared by many of the production workers) while, on the other hand, most of the firm's senior executives admired her for her unshakeable determination in resisting union pressures and demands. It therefore came as little surprise to the management team, but as something of a shock to everyone else, when, within months of her appointment, the personnel manager was prematurely retired and she was appointed to the post.

While, as previously stated, Parkinson-Browne is unmarried, she does not go short of male company and, in fact, has progressed through a series of friendships and liaisons with members of the opposite sex. Essentially extrovert by nature, she tends to 'stick out in a crowd' and can be relied upon to contribute much to the success of almost any social occasion. Christened 'Iron Annie' by her personnel staff, she is generally regarded by them as a classic exponent of Women's Lib and, perhaps more to the point, as someone with whom it might be unwise to cross swords. She constantly ensures that her staff of eleven men and women (previously fourteen, but reduced to eleven by way of one redundancy and two dismissals for inefficiency) work effectively and hard and, as often observed by her managing director, she is loth to suffer fools gladly.

Parkinson-Browne is a smoker and, although she does not hesitate to drink socially, positively detests and roundly condemns any degree of over-indulgence in alcohol. Tending to lead conversations rather than merely interject comments, she needs little encouragement to speak volubly and well on almost any topic.

Now, here is what I would like you to do. On the basis of information available in the report, record your responses to the following questions by circling the appropriate number in each case, or making a note on a separate piece of paper.

Patricia Parkinson-Browne – assessment

		Low					High
1	How do you rate this person's overall sense of duty?	1	2	3	4	5	6
2	How do you rate this person's suitability as a 'manager of people'?	1	2	3	4	5	6
3	Assume that you are required to *work alongside* this person. How would you rate your chances of achieving a generally satisfactory working relationship?	1	2	3	4	5	6
4	Assume that you are required to *work under* this person. How would you rate your chances of achieving respect for her as your boss?	1	2	3	4	5	6

5   Assume that you are required to be this
    person's *boss*. How would you rate her
    chances of meeting generally with the
    standards you impose on your
    subordinates?   1 2 3 4 5 6

                                             Badly   Very well

6   Finally, how do you think this person
    would 'get on' with your real-life staff? 1 2 3 4 5 6

If you have any burning comments to make, jot them down
on your paper. We'll return to Patricia Parkinson-Browne in a
jiffy.

WORKBOX CRIB BANK

Teaser 1

Although the list can be well-nigh endless, you've probably
written down such qualities as:

- Integrity   • Job knowledge
- Enthusiasm   • Job proficiency
- Common sense   • Ability to communicate
- Resourcefulness   • Ability to inspire loyalty
- Reliability   • Sense of duty
- Cooperation   • Appearance and bearing

Anyway, whatever qualities you have chosen, I'd like you
to consider them in the light of this question: 'To what extent
do you think such undoubted leaders as Attila the Hun, Joseph
Stalin, Adolf Hitler and Benito Mussolini fit your mould?'
Since I do not wish to be landed with a suit for libel, I must ask
you to cast your eyes round today's world of work and come
up with your own live equivalents to the devils I've
mentioned. They're certainly there, are they not – that
singular breed of arrogant, people-crushing, *eminently successful* captains of industry. So, does this not pose a second
question? Why do those who preach about leadership tend to
insist that the person at the helm must possess all of the virtues
and, ideally, none of the vices?

Think about this, will you? I'll return to the point in the crib
bank at the end of Chapter 2.

Teaser 2

Yes, you're right, this paper exercise is just about as far removed from reality as it is possible to get – or is it? Certainly, the one big snag is that you were required to assess Patricia without the colossal benefit of her physical presence and, in terms of perception of the individual, you were thus mightily inhibited. But you were provided with a lot of information – quite enough to enable you to answer most, if not all, of the questions.

Now, this is where I must ask you to believe a flat statement. I've given this task of assessing Patricia Parkinson-Browne to a fair old number of managers and others and, here's the crunch, the results have always varied like the March winds. To state the rather obvious, your perception of Patricia *or anyone else*, will be significantly different to that of Tom, Myrtle, Dick or Harriet. In fact, when I scan the accumulated results, I might just as well have thrown a dice the requisite number of times – the overall outcome would have been exactly the same.

All of which raises a pertinent question – if we all view people differently, who is right? Is your perception of one of your juniors right – *or is it up the creek*?

I've subjected you to quite a bit of work in order to make my point but, being the devil I am, I make no apology. If it's any comfort, we'll be dealing with the way you perceive your subordinates in some detail later on – so just regard this exercise as a kind of early preamble, okay?

2 But am I really like that?

A CANDID SELF-APPRAISAL OF PERSONAL STRENGTHS AND WEAKNESSES

Many moons ago, a thoroughly autocratic boss-acquaintance of mine took himself off to one of the up-and-coming 'executive assessment centres' – the type of spell-binding place where, in exchange for a small fortune, candidates are stripped to the mental buff and probed for their good and not-so-good attributes as managers. Having been duly assessed, he returned to his working bailiwick, brandishing a four-page report on the state of his executive health and swearing that, by hook or by crook, he'd mend his management ways.

Take my word for it, the blighter didn't. To this day, he remains a pig's orphan of a boss – head of a failing business, heartily detested by his come-and-swiftly-go employees and, if looks are anything to go by, long overdue for the coronary that'll carry him off.

Which, of course, brings me to the subject of this chapter. To put it in a nutshell, it's just like that long-forgotten peepshow proprietor said, 'You pays your money and you takes your choice.' If, perchance, you are a leopard with super-indelible spots – well, if I were you, I'd do anything rather than waste my time on that which follows. Please don't splutter that you haven't been warned.

A MANAGEMENT QUESTIONNAIRE

Plainly, there are two possible approaches to this little exercise. You can either complete it with twenty-four carat honesty or, of course, you can set out to lie through your pearly teeth. Lest you are tempted to indulge in a spot of mental chicanery, suffice it to say that the Great Chairman in the Sky has a beady eye for porkie pies and, more to the point, a mighty long memory.

It's quite straightforward. Record your considered reaction to each statement below by ticking the most appropriate alternative. By the way, just in case you have no wish to deface the exercise, itself, you'll find some additional 'response columns' at the back of the book.

Right, then, off we go.

1   The oft-professed belief that a manager should regard himself as the captain of a team is unrealistic – work is not a game.

- I agree – it's pure claptrap.   (. . .) 1
- I disagree – it makes sense.   (. . .) 2

2   It is possible to make almost any job more stimulating and challenging.

- I agree – and a manager should always strive to this end.   (. . .) 3
- I disagree – the statement takes little account of reality at the sharp end.   (. . .) 4

3   A manager should hold regular 'hair-down' sessions at work – at which all members of staff should be encouraged to air their views, even when these clash with his own, deeply-held beliefs.

- I agree – there is little to fear and potentially much to gain from these healthy exercises in communication.   (. . .) 5
- They may be all right for some, but in my situation there just isn't the time for such luxuries.   (. . .) 6
- I disagree – such meetings represent little other than a potentially dangerous charter for barrack-room lawyers and troublemakers.   (. . .) 7

4   One disadvantage of delegation is that it tends to make subordinates feel more important.

- Yes, this is an unfortunate fact and, unless one's careful, I think there's a distinct risk that one's authority can be undermined. (. . .) 8
- Right or wrong, it matters little. (. . .) 9
- Rubbish – motivation-wise, this is one of the great *advantages* of delegation. (. . .) 10

5   A first priority in management is to constantly ensure that all subordinates obey the firm's rules and regulations.

- I agree wholeheartedly. Without constant vigilance in this regard, disciplined work and conduct would swiftly go by the board and then where would we be? (. . .) 11
- I think this statement is way over the top. The effective manager will have no need to *constantly* check that people are obeying the rules – given good leadership, the vast majority of them will behave themselves, anyway. (. . .) 12
- This is just another textbook pontification – telling me something I already know. (. . .) 13

6   The average employee likes to be directed and prefers not to have responsibility.

- Yes, whether we're conscious of it or not, most of us like to be told what's what – and life's certainly brighter without the burden of responsibility. (. . .) 14
- Tosh. The average employee thrives on good leadership, but he also appreciates having a say in what he does at work. What's more, he enjoys rising to the challenges inherent in shouldering his fair share of responsibility. (. . .) 15

7   The competent manager will never require a subordinate to perform any task that he cannot do himself.

- I agree – this is the mark of a good
  manager.   (. . .) 16
- I disagree – this is the classic cry of the
  unthinking, gung-ho type of manager. (. . .) 17

8 A manager should constantly strive to maintain a
friendly working atmosphere by giving attention to
subordinates' needs for satisfying team relationships.

- So what's such a manager supposed to be
  doing – running a social club?   (. . .) 18
- I can't say I disagree, but in the real world
  it isn't that simple.   (. . .) 19
- I fully agree.   (. . .) 20

9 The manager who has a good knowledge of his subordinates has no real need to conduct 'performance
against objectives' counselling sessions.

- I agree, if he only has a few subordinates,
  he'll be more than familiar with their
  performance – and their strengths and
  weaknesses.   (. . .) 21
- I disagree. There is always a need for such
  sessions – if only to literally force the
  manager into taking a formal and
  comprehensive survey of each individual's progress, successes and hang-ups.
  Besides which, subordinates derive
  considerable value from appraisal
  counselling – provided it's done
  properly.   (. . .) 22

10 The essence of effective management is that the manager
gives orders – he alone decides what has to be done and,
while he may or may not consider his subordinates'
feelings about a given task, they are required to obey.

- I agree – good, firm management.   (. . .) 23
- I disagree – a bit too much of the iron heel
  for my liking.   (. . .) 24

11 A subordinate's pride in his work is, in itself, an
important reward.

- So, big deal – some have pride in their work, many don't. This is just another pie-in-the-sky pontification from one of those ivory tower egg-heads. (. . .) 25
- I fully agree. (. . .) 26

12 Delegation is simply the act of passing on to a subordinate some aspect of the work that a manager is required to do.

- I agree – that's it. (. . .) 27
- No, there's a great deal more to delegation than that. (. . .) 28

13 An effective manager will frequently stress the need for all members of his team to be ahead of work schedules.

- I disagree – an effective manager will have no need to do this. (. . .) 29
- I agree. It's a manager's job to motivate people to make a greater effort – and this is part-and-parcel of that motivation. (. . .) 30

14 The vast majority of employees learn, under proper conditions, not only to accept but to seek challenging work.

- I agree. (. . .) 31
- I disagree. (. . .) 32

15 For optimum results in problem-solving, a manager defines the problem and the limits within which the decision must be made – his subordinates then work on the problem and decide as a group what to do.

- No, this is not my cup of tea. (. . .) 33
- I agree – it's a sound generalization. (. . .) 34

16 The best way a manager can develop a subordinate's competence is by maintaining a high flow of delegated tasks, thereby keeping up the pressure on him to improve his performance.

- I agree – always provided, of course, that the level of pressure maintained is fair and reasonable. (. . .) 35

- No, I do not think this is the best way to
  develop someone's competence.   (. . .) 36

17   The wise manager will regularly remind subordinates that their jobs are dependent on the firm's ability to compete successfully.

- I disagree. This type of cracking the whip
  is old-hat, counter-productive and drives
  a horse and cart through good manage-
  ment practice.   (. . .) 37
- I agree – keeps them on their toes.   (. . .) 38

18   In the event that a manager has any visitors to his bailiwick, he should always ensure that he, and he alone, deals with them on behalf of his team.

- In some instances, yes – in all instances,
  no.   (. . .) 39
- I agree – this way there can be no
  mistaken impressions or other gaffes.   (. . .) 40

19   The effective leader sets goals, determines policies and lays plans; discloses only sufficient of his plans and intentions to allow subordinates to perform their current tasks; determines what, how and when work should be done and who does what; preserves his position by remaining aloof from his team.

- This definition broadly represents my
  approach to leadership.   (. . .) 41
- This definition does not reflect my
  approach to leadership.   (. . .) 42

20   A manager should ensure efficiency by arranging his subordinates' work in such a way that human elements and relationships present minimal problems.

- I agree – always provided that work
  requirements remain a manager's
  number one priority.   (. . .) 43
- Here we go again. No, I disagree entirely
  – this statement just about sums up
  what's wrong in business and industry
  today.   (. . .) 44

21   A manager should foster good working relationships by ridding his team of those who don't fit in.

- If this means that quick bullets should be fired without even making an effort to change the attitudes (etc.) of those concerned – then I disagree entirely.   (. . .) 45
- I agree. When building a team, it's far better to concentrate one's efforts where they'll yield results – not waste them on rotten apples.   (. . .) 46

22   While the proficient manager will take the initiative in making decisions, he is always willing to entertain his subordinates' views before finally making up his mind – and will change it if they offer a better alternative.

- Yes, I agree with this one.   (. . .) 47
- I disagree – such discussion or what-have-you is often fruitless and, in any event, leads to almost inevitable delay in the decision-making process.   (. . .) 48

23   The hapless manager is beset on all sides by uninformed and impracticable do-gooders who, by dint of advice and onerous legislation, conspire to make his already complicated job a misery.

- My sentiments, exactly. Why can't we be left alone to get on with what we're (barely) paid to do – manage?   (. . .) 49
- I hope the person who uttered this nonsense isn't a manager – for if he is, I pity the poor creatures who are under him.   (. . .) 50
- Look, I'm all for being taught 'good management', because that'll make me better at my job – what I can't stand is the manner in which current employment legislation restricts me from carrying it out.   (. . .) 51

24   All the pundits seem to reject what they call autocratic or authoritarian leadership yet, if they take the trouble to look around, it'll be perfectly apparent to them that

many so-called 'captains of industry' are the very hard-nuts they seek to condemn.

- Again, my sentiments, exactly. One of the main troubles with today's society, in general, is an almost total lack of discipline – and a namby-pamby approach to management at work doesn't help one little bit. (. . .) 52

- Whoever said this is talking rubbish. One doesn't have to be authoritarian to be a good leader – quite simply, that's management by coercion or fear. (. . .) 53

- To hell with all the theorizing, I'm not interested. I just wish to be left alone to get on with my job. (. . .) 54

25   Work is a jungle where dog-eat-dog is the order of the day. Like it or not, it's the back-stabbers and the chosen few who live to tell the tale, and this fight for sheer survival leaves precious little time for the niceties of good management.

- Yes, that just about says it all. If I don't look after myself, no one else will – so, for my money, it's Number One that counts. (. . .) 55

- Twaddle. I've sufficient faith in myself and others to believe that, by and large, my efforts will stand me in good stead. Sure, I'm not blind – these days, no one can be totally secure and, yes, I do have my fair share of doubts and hang-ups. But I do my level best to manage my people without fear or favour – from anyone. (. . .) 56

Well, now, that's the first round over and done with, but before we examine your responses, let's be gluttons for punishment and tackle another little exercise.

A SPOT OF CANDID INTROSPECTION

It's disarmingly simple. Merely place a tick against any of the following 'character traits' that most closely reflect inclinations-cum-aspects of your own personality. Once again, I need hardly add that utter self-candour is necessary if you're not to waste your time.

Turn to the back of the book for further copies of the list.

I have a distinct tendency to be:

- Moody   (. . .)
- Touchy   (. . .)
- Sociable   (. . .)
- Passive   (. . .)
- Anxious   (. . .)
- Restless   (. . .)
- Outgoing   (. . .)
- Careful   (. . .)
- Rigid   (. . .)
- Aggressive   (. . .)
- Talkative   (. . .)
- Thoughtful   (. . .)
- Sober*   (. . .)
- Excitable   (. . .)
- Responsive   (. . .)
- Peaceful   (. . .)
- Pessimistic   (. . .)
- Changeable   (. . .)
- Easygoing   (. . .)
- Controlled   (. . .)
- Reserved   (. . .)
- Impulsive   (. . .)
- Lively   (. . .)
- Reliable   (. . .)
- Unsociable   (. . .)
- Optimistic   (. . .)
- Carefree   (. . .)

*Sober-minded you understand – not the other.

- Even-tempered   (. . .)
- Quiet   (. . .)
- Active   (. . .)
- Leaderly   (. . .)
- Calm   (. . .)

That wasn't so bad, was it? We'll be returning to this second exercise in a minute but, right now, it's time that we got to grips with your responses to the initial set of statements.

Management questionnaire – gathering the strings together

As you've probably guessed, you are required to transfer your personal selection of responses in line with what follows but, before you start, here's a stern *caveat* for your digestion. The whole object of the questionnaire is to provide you with triggers for thought – unlike those quiz-type features so favoured by the Sunday rag-sheets, it does not purport to provide you with a blow-by-blow analysis of your inner self. So, bearing in mind that we're concerned with *indicative clues* as to your management style and what-not, let's get on with it.

Question One: *Do you tend to be authoritative or consultative/participative when managing your subordinates?*

Listed below are some of the response numbers. By cross-referring to the questionaire, ring *only* those numbers which you happened to tick and then 'block in' one segment on the *authoritative scale* for each number you have ringed.

Note, again, that you will find further copies of all this at the back of the book.

    7   11   18   23   25   27   30   33
    35   38   41   44   46   48   49   52

Now do exactly the same in respect of the following response numbers but, this time, 'block in' segments on the *consultative/participative scale*.

    2   5   12   15   20   22   24   28
    36   37   42   43   45   47   50   53

Authoritative scale ‹‹‹‹

█ ▌☐☐☐☐☐☐☐☐☐☐☐☐☐☐☐☐☐

Consultative/participative scale ‹‹‹‹

█ ☐☐☐☐☐☐☐☐☐☐☐☐☐☐☐☐☐☐

Post-mortem

I'm no mathematician, but I believe there's a reasonable chance that your scales will depict a trend to either an authoritarian or consultative/participative style of management. However, if, perchance, you've come up with anything like a 'fifty-fifty' result, you're still not out of the woods; for, of course, this can indicate a likely vacillation in management style and that, alone, is food for thought, isn't it?

I think it behoves us to remind ourselves exactly what is meant by these textbook terms 'authoritative' and 'consultative/participative':

- *The authoritarian manager*: Here we have the manager who, relishing his position of power over subordinates, utilizes that power to the full by taking unilateral decisions, telling his flock only that which he considers it is necessary for them to be told (a thorough misuse of the 'need to know' principle) and, if we're not to mince matters, getting things done by the simple process of coercion. Harsh words? Well, yes, but if the cap fits, reader. . . . One thing is for certain, if your responses are slanted in favour of an authoritarian approach, you can be sure that your subordinates view you in a *much* more positive light. It's a pretty safe bet that, in their ultra-perceptive eyes, you're little short of being a brass-bound, hard-as-nails, autocratic so-and-so. More on this anon.
- *The consultative/participative manager*: If, on the other hand, you have emerged from the questionnaire with an honest inclination to the consultative/participative style – well, praise be! The manager who has this magic essence flowing abundantly in his or her executive veins is the person who, taking full advantage of the consultation process without losing a scrap of authority, makes

decisions and stands by them. This is the manager who encourages participation, especially by means of effective delegation but never at the price of diminished personal authority. It can be said that the one hundred per cent consultative/participative boss has attained nirvana – if you like, a true state of management grace. Again, more of this rare quality anon.

Question Two: *How do you stand in the motivation stakes?*

Listed below are two further batches of response numbers (yes, some of which have been utilized in Question One). Again, ring only those which you happened to tick and 'block in' the appropriate number of segments on each of the two scales.

Motivation plus scale
3 5 10 15 20 22 26 28 29 31 38 47

Motivation minus scale
1 4 6 14 18 21 25 27 30 32 37 48

Motivation plus scale «««

■											

Motivation minus scale «««

■											

Post-mortem

Motivation – in good management, the vital art of impelling employees to willing and enthusiastic action. Now, clearly, there's no way that the questionnaire can establish the actual degree of your success as a motivator. If you'll forgive the repetition, all we're concerned with is identifying your 'management leanings' and, in this section, whether or not you tend to have a *positive* attitude to motivation. Well, now – do you?

Needless to add, we'll be returning again and again to the question of motivation throughout the ensuing chapters.

Question Three: *How 'secure' – how 'confident' – are you as a manager?*

Same drill – ring the response numbers you have ticked and complete the two scales, accordingly.

Security/confidence plus scale
5   10   12   16   22   29   33   37   39   56
Security/confidence minus scale
8   11   14   19   21   30   34   38   40   55

Security/confidence plus scale «««

■□□□□□□□□□

Security/confidence minus scale «««

■□□□□□□□□□

Post-mortem
It's at this point that I start planting my size elevens in a very dodgy minefield. If you do tend to feel insecure, if you do lack confidence in your ability to weather the company maelstrom and manage people effectively, probably the last thing you need is a total stranger, author-chappie who seems hell-bent on rubbing the salt in. For, let's face it, if you have come up with a negative result, that's just about all that this questionnaire has achieved.

Or is it? Is there, I wonder, the faintest chance that, this time, you will be triggered into earnest and constructive thought about your unfortunately common predicament? If so, the last chapter in this book is intended for your very quiet and private attention.

Having stated thus, there is the other side of the coin to consider. If you've scored a roaring success in this security/confidence aspect, never forget the ever-present threat of those monstrous twins, *false* security and arrant *over*confidence. They're the stealthy advance guard of management Nemesis – and you'd better believe it.

Question Four: *What about apathy – laissez faire?*
Take heart, this is the final section – check if you have ticked

any of the following responses and complete the scale, accordingly.

Apathy/laissez faire scale «««

4   9   13   17   19   27   51   54   55

Apathy/laissez faire scale «««

Post-mortem

Let's try to be realistic. I consider it highly unlikely that anyone who is thoroughly steeped in apathy/laissez faire will even pick up this book, let alone take the trouble to read it – and if I'm anywhere near right, this last section is kicked straight into touch. But, bearing in mind that we're concerned with triggers for thought, what about the chance that you, reader, opted to skip through the entire questionnaire without any attempt at thinking things over? Assuming that you're reading this little chunk (which, I admit, is a pretty optimistic assumption) could your lack of interest spring from apathetic/laissez faire roots?

And, if this is the case, what do you imagine your juniors think of your weakness – which will have become evident to them in umpteen different ways? Make no mistake, in the eagle eyes of your subordinates, your shortcomings stand out like neon signs. *They know* what makes you tick, and they can see Nemesis poised above your head long before she swoops.

I hope you found the questionnaire of some use in stimulating your thoughts about the manner in which you approach this thorny business of management. That said, I'd now like to return to the second little exercise.

A spot of candid introspection

You'll recall that you placed a tick against those of the listed 'character traits' which most closely resemble aspects of your own personality. Right, now transfer your ticks to the appropriate spaces in Figure 1.

Unstable

( ) Moody   Touchy ( )
( ) Anxious   Restless ( )
( ) Rigid   Aggressive ( )
( ) Sober   Excitable ( )
( ) Pessimistic   Changeable ( )
( ) Reserved   Impulsive ( )
( ) Unsociable   Optimistic ( )
( ) Quiet   Active ( )

Introverted   **Extroverted**

( ) Passive   Sociable ( )
( ) Careful   Outgoing ( )
( ) Thoughtful   Talkative ( )
( ) Even-tempered   Responsive ( )
( ) Controlled   Easygoing ( )
( ) Reliable   Leaderly ( )
( ) Peaceful   Carefree ( )
( ) Calm   Lively ( )

Stable

Figure 1
(*Source:* Eysenck H. J., *Fact and Fiction in Psychology*, Penguin, 1965.
Reproduced by permission of Penguin Books Ltd)

Post-mortem

Since it's not my wish to shove you headlong into the complex waters of psychology (where, believe you me, yours truly is a complete non-swimmer) we'll keep things on a very basic level. That said, the chart in Figure 1 illustrates one aspect of modern psychological research which I think you'll agree has some practical relevance to the question of management style; namely, the widely accepted theory that an individual's personality can be *more or less* stable and *more or less* extrovert. But do regard these four, highly emotive terms – unstable, stable, introvert and extrovert – with caution!

Note that we are concerned with trends, not absolutes – for very few people are one hundred per cent introvert or one hundred per cent extrovert. Plainly, the distribution of your ticks within the four quarters of the chart will provide an *indication* of your 'personal trend(s)', and, hopefully, this may help you to know yourself better and, of course, enable you to examine your particular management style in greater depth.

Finally, it's worth remembering that in no sense is the extrovert 'better' or 'worse' than the introvert – being human, they are merely different. While an extrovert may certainly find it easier to rub shoulders with other folk and be the life and soul of the party, he may also be far too unreliable and impulsive to make a good manager.

A FINAL DIG IN THE RIBS

By now, you shouldn't need me to remind you that your personal management style is almost certainly *the* primary determinant of your success or failure at this most difficult of tasks. So – physician, heal thyself!

WORKBOX NUMBER 2

Teaser 1
This little task will require more than a smidgen of dedication. Select your most able subordinate and, placing yourself in his or her head, write a summary of how, given all the evidence at your disposal, this person views you as a manager. It's absolutely vital for the success of this exercise that you effectively gag your own, private opinions of yourself and concentrate like anything on expressing what, to the best of your knowledge and intuition, your junior thinks of you.

Remember, we're after a written summary, not just the odd higgledy-piggledy word or two.

Teaser 2
You'll maybe agree that one very good method of fanning motivation in one's subordinates is to positively encourage them to come up with innovative ideas and proposals and then let them see that their respective brainchilds are receiving positive consideration.

Unfortunately, there's one huge potential snag in all this – one that puts all other possible difficulties in the shade. Please put your finger on it, will you?

WORKBOX CRIB BANK

Teaser 1

It's possible that you're not going to like this – because what I'm going to suggest (unfortunately, I cannot instruct) will test the strength of your relationship with that chosen subordinate. It's simply this: present the person with your written summary and ask him or her to tell you, with no beating round the bush, exactly what he/she thinks of this pen-picture of you as a manager. There's no need to admit that it's how you imagined their thoughts would run but, plainly, you can if you so wish.

Now, having read that, I fancy you will be prey to one of three reactions:

'Oh, all right, I'll give it to so-and-so and see what he/she thinks. . . .'
'It's not worth the candle.'
'No fear – what do you take me for?'

Here are my replies – pick whichever is relevant:

- *First alternative*: Good. You should find the exercise interesting and informative – especially if you remember that appraisal by one's subordinate is far more accurate than by any other means.
- *Second alternative*: You lazy creature, you – why, I don't expect you've even taken the trouble to write the summary. Alternatively, does this reaction provide a solid indication that your relationship with your chosen (quote) 'most able subordinate' positively stinks; or is it simply the case that you lack faith in your written summary – or your junior? Or, bringing the wheel full circle, *are* you just plain lazy – in which case, my old china, why don't you go and watch Andy Pandy instead of reading this stuff? And resign?

Teaser 2

The principle of fanning motivation by encouraging subordinates to come up with innovative ideas is sound, indeed.

The huge potential snag in all this is – you! All right, I did say *'potential* snag' but, apart from agreeing that the principle's a good one, what have you *actually done* to encourage your juniors to thus exercise their minds?

In addition to the lethargy that simmers in the veins of far too many managers (present company excepted), there's the well-proven fact that 'ideas from below' are often viewed with disfavour and even fear by some executives – if only for the reason that they didn't think of them, themselves. You know the attitude – heavens, they'll be feeding them meat next, and then where will we be?

The moral must be, don't just think about it – be innovative, and get those ideas coming!

Leaders and leadership

As promised in Workbox Number 1 here is a bit more on this topic.

You recall that I posed the question: Why do those who preach about effective management and what-all tend to insist that a leader should possess all the 'goodie' qualities and, ideally, none of the more unpleasant traits? And, yes, the answer is strikingly obvious, as is the clue to enlightenment enshrined in that one word, 'ideally' – for, regardless of how far it may be over the horizon, we must always pursue the Holy Grail of (note the qualification) *near*-perfection. The thoroughly autocratic, aggressive, self-centred leader may well get to the top of his chosen tree but, as I implied earlier, he'll tread on many, many necks to get there. Contrary to what these self-same people usually think, this form of success is miles removed from good, let alone near-perfect, leadership.

'Rubbish – absolute rubbish. In getting to where I am today, I've brought prosperity to a previously ailing company and, just in case you've overlooked the point, created jobs for many people who, had it not been for my efforts, would probably still be on the dole. I tell you, I'm heartily sick of this sanctimonious claptrap – instead of practising your totally unrealistic, bleeding-hearts brand of evangelism, why don't you match my record? The honest truth is, you haven't got what it takes. . . .'

Apart from leaving you with a thought, I'm going to invite you to answer that broadside. The thought is this: could you live easily with your conscience if you practised this full-blown, autocratic brand of leadership? If your reaction is in the affirmative – why, your honoured place in Hades is assured, ready and waiting.

3 Now, what are they really like?

GETTING AT THE TRUTH OF HOW AND WHY EMPLOYEES TICK AS THEY DO

If there's one question that I've tossed with monotonous frequency at manager-chums and colleagues over the years, it just has to be that deliberately casual leg-spinner, 'Tell me, how well do you know your subordinates?' You can probably guess the general tenor of the replies; like:

- 'Pretty well, I'd say – after all, one can't manage a group of people for very long without getting to know them as individuals, can one?'
- 'Huh, I know them all right and, what's more, I bear the scars to prove it.'
- 'Look, it's my job to recognize their personal strengths and weaknesses and, since you ask, I reckon I'm fairly good at the game.'
- 'Put it this way – i always make a practice of getting to know everyone on my team. Isn't this what management's all about?'

The point is, with the exception of those who told me that they were new in the post and hadn't had time to get to know their worthy juniors, I'm unable to recall a single instance when someone admitted to less than adequate knowledge; which, at first glance, would seem to kick the purpose of this chapter straight into touch. But does it? In order to whet your appetite, let's start again – this time, with an invitation.

> *Clive Goodworth*
> *requests the pleasure of your company*
> *at the dissection*
> *of a selected subordinate*
> *right here and now!*
> *Please bring your*   *Black Tie and*
> *victim with you*   *Theatre Gown*

Thanks for coming! Now, first of all and to be quite serious, I'm assuming that you profess to have a goodly knowledge of your chosen subordinate. This is important, because, once we've popped the poor creature on the slab, we're going to wield our shared scalpel and put your knowledge to the test. I'll plunge the knife in – you fish around and come up with the honest answers, okay? Oh, yes, and do consider each item at some length. Imagine, if you like, that on pain of flaming death you're required to supply reasoned, in-depth responses and we'll see how you fare.

I AM THIS PERSON'S BOSS
AND, IF I'M GOOD AT MY JOB,
I SHOULD KNOW A GREAT DEAL
ABOUT THIS SUBORDINATE

BUT DO I?

1   What is the true extent of my familiarity with this person's previous job history?

2   What is my considered view of the manner in which his/ her career progressed prior to joining us? To what extent does this progression reflect a well-motivated, planned career?

3   What about this person's present job? On due thought, to what extent does this represent a logical step in terms of good career planning?

4   If I were required to make detailed comment on this

subordinate's readiness to accept responsibilities at work, what would I say and how would I justify my observations?

5   Similarly, if I was required to report on this person's general common sense, both in and out of work, what would I say and, again, how would I justify my views?

6   And what about cooperation? What would I have to say about the quality of his/her teamwork, and why?

7   And general reliability? What would I have to say about this, and why?

8   What is my considered view of this subordinate's overall appearance and bearing, as measured against others performing a similar role?

9   What is my assessment of the quality and depth of his/her job knowledge – again, as measured against others performing a similar role?

10   If I were required to make detailed comment on this person's resourcefulness at work, what would I say and why?

11   And what would I have to say about his/her overall job proficiency and how would I justify my views?

12   How would I be inclined to describe this subordinate's overriding motivation at work?

- Would I say that he/she is mainly preoccupied with maximizing earnings and if so, how would I justify such a generalization?

- Or, on thinking it over, would I say that this person's main concern is for sheer continuity of employment – to the extent that he/she will avoid making any kind of waves that might threaten this compulsive yen for security? If so, how would I justify this opinion?

- Or, albeit that this employee may attach due importance to money and job security, would I say that he/she tends to place a noticeable priority on the business of achieving successful working relationships i.e. making a distinct effort to be accepted, to 'belong', to identify with his/her colleagues? If so, how would I justify such a generalization?

- Or do I conclude that this subordinate attaches great

importance to such things as gaining recognition, prestige or status in my eyes and/or in the eyes of his/her peers and subordinates? If so, how would I justify this generalization?

- Or would I say that this person stands out as an all-round, competent achiever – constantly seeking new challenges and exhibiting zest in his/her work? If so, how would I justify this generalization?
- Or exactly what would I say and why?

13 If I were required to make detailed comment on this employee's hobbies and leisure activities, what would I say in terms of listing the various activities and describing his/her level of interest and involvement in each one?

14 If this person lives with a partner, what can I say about the quality of the relationship and any knock-on effect this may have on his/her working life? What instances can I bring to mind to support my views?

15 What can I say of substance regarding the general stability of this employee's life outside work and how would I justify my comments?

16 Following on from 14 and 15, above, is this person saddled with any other complications or problems; such as:

- Defects of personality?
- Financial troubles?
- Accommodation difficulties?
- Trouble with children?
- Personal or family illness/disability?
- Personal or family alcohol/drug abuse?

What are my considered views and, again, how would I justify them?

So, there we are. How did you get on with that little lot? Be honest, did you just skim through the sixteen items or, very hopefully, did you actually engage in some hard thought and put your knowledge of your selected junior to the test? All I can say is, in the event that you opted for the easy way out, I suggest that you skip the next few paragraphs for they're likely to bore you rigid.

No, I did exactly as I was bid – what now?
Well, before dealing with your responses to the questionnaire, I'd like to be a trifle devious and quiz you on your
selection of a guinea pig subordinate. You see, human nature
being what it is, I'm wondering if you just happened to choose
the member of your team who, for good or ill, is best known
to you – I mean, there's nearly always one of them who
springs most nimbly to mind. If you did put your finger on
this attractively soft option, the odds are that you sailed
through the exercise with minimal trouble but, in so doing,
scored a somewhat spurious victory. The big question is, if
you forced yourself to repeat the quiz in respect of *each and
every one* of your juniors, would you still come up so thickly
covered in glory?

> 'Er, be that as it may . . . I'm more concerned with the
> message you're trying to put over – which, I might add, is
> a pretty obvious one. Of course, managers need to have
> knowledge of their subordinates and, frankly, I don't
> need reminding of the fact. For goodness sake, let's get
> on.'

I've no means of telling whether that mini-outburst
represents your views, reader, but if it does, stand by for a
broadside riposte. The stark fact is that very few managers
who control, say, five or more people can lay true claim to
really comprehensive knowledge of each individual. And lest
I've failed to make the point, it's in-depth knowledge of the
whole individual that counts, not just his or her working
persona. To hell with the warning signs, I'm about to clamber
way out on the rotten old limb of controversy.

I am absolutely convinced and, if necessary, I'd like to
convince you that it's a manager's bounden duty to become a
quietly efficient intelligence agent (or, if you prefer a more
emotive term, Paul Pry) where his juniors are concerned.
Quite simply, he should make it his business to grow ears the
size of Dumbo's redoubtable lugs and he should use these
flapping antennae in conjunction with his eyes to pick up every
odd transmission that chances to burble over the workplace
wavelength. To the extent, mark you, that:

the three words uttered by Mary to her chum over a cuppa on Tuesday morning, being duly overheard and remembered, can be linked to her casual comment to no one in particular on Friday – thereby providing a valuable, composite clue that her workaday world is overshadowed, say, by trouble at home;

when passing John's desk, you note that an obviously private telephone call is causing him some embarrassed disquiet. From your snapshot eavesdropping on a single comment, it would seem that he is trying to ward off a debt collector and, pondering on this snippet of probability, you recall his earlier, seemingly casual query about the chances of working overtime. Just perhaps, you are one step on the way to discovering why John normally a bright and breezy worker, has been somewhat withdrawn of late;

since your ears pick up unusual silences, too, you observe that young Susie, normally an attractive extrovert, now appears to clam up when Monday morning chit-chat gets round to the subject of what everyone did with themselves at the weekend. And, come to think of it, it's been some time since she last mentioned her fiancé in casual conversation, which is most uncharacteristic. Is there trouble at t'mill?

etc. etc.

That's torn it – Nosey Parker management – whatever happened to civil liberties and the hallowed maxim that what an employee does after the knell of cease-work is his own private affair? Good grief, I hear you say, it'll be Big Brother next.

Well, controversial or not, I stick by my guns and urge you to get out there and exercise your executive inquisitiveness to the full. Kenneth Grahame nearly said it:

> Know all about them that there is to be knowed
> – *before* the event

However, prior to leaping into action, do note that there are a couple of inviolable ground rules:

- *Never* use your garnered intelligence on members of staff for other than filing in your own ultra-private, mental dossiers. The boss who fuels the flames of management tittle-tattle with such information is a turncoat and a rogue.
- *Never* get found out! Once you are identified as a nosing hear-all and see-all – why, you're dead.

Let's now return to the questionnaire and dig up some comment regarding the sixteen items.

Questions 1, 2 and 3

The knowledge that Joe Entwhistle's previous job history is outlined within his deeply-filed application for employment does *not* constitute personal familiarity with the guy's past endeavours. Similarly, a vague, assumption-ridden notion of the drives, circumstances and decisions which, in sum, engineered this progression is no substitute for a comprehensive insight into his ability to plan and mould a career. .

- Why and how did Joe come to be what he is now, job-wise?
- What strengths and weaknesses of planning and general character are thus highlighted?
- What can be done in terms of capitalizing on/eradicating these revealed past strengths and weaknesses so far as his present job is concerned?

Questions 4 to 11, inclusive

Yes, these questions smack of the type to be found within almost any staff assessment form and if you are required to formally appraise your people, you could be excused for tossing this familiar selection lightly aside. But hold on, with or without the benefit of any experience in appraisal, put yourself to the test.

First, to save you digging back, the questions deal with the following personal traits:

- Readiness to accept responsibility
- General common sense

- Cooperation
- Reliability
- Overall appearance and bearing
- Quality and depth of job knowledge
- Resourcefulness
- Overall job proficiency

All right, with the possible exception of 'overall appearance and bearing', could you write *at least a full page of objective narrative report on each item* in respect of each of your subordinates – complete with detailed examples of conduct and/or performance to justify your findings?

What's that – of course, you could? Well, here's a cheeky chappie who isn't exactly encouraged by your oh-so-swift rejoinder; so why not prove him wrong by writing up just one person – to wit, the least considered of your team?

Question 12
If you've had any training in the principles of management, it's a fair old bet that this question will have prompted you to growl 'Oh, no – not Maslow, *again*.' – or words to that effect. Albeit that A. H. Maslow's Hierarchy of Human Needs (or, if you like, theory of human motivation) is often one of the least attractive pills to be thrust down trainees' throats, albeit that it's been branded as oversimplistic – the wise manager will never forget that it makes a great deal of sense.

According to Maslow, we each of us are driven throughout our lives by five levels of need, organized in a hierarchy or ladder of importance. These levels of need are, lowest first:

- *Physiological needs*: These are the vital, basic needs for shelter, rest, food and drink etc. While, very fortunately, most of us manage to ascend beyond this lowest rung on Maslow's ladder, it behoves us to remember that all are not so blessed by fate.
- *Safety/security needs*: These are the needs that drive us to seek protection from the dangers and threats of life – thus, for instance, we strive to so organize things as best we can that the future holds minimum peril for us and our loved

ones. Things like savings, insurance policies and pension schemes spring to mind.

- *Social needs*:   If we are mentally healthy (and perish any thought to the contrary) we are next driven by the needs for friendships, acceptance by social and work groups, etc. It's an obvious point, but herein lies the indictment of such horrors as solitary confinement and the thankfully well-nigh extinct trade union practice, as they say, of sending some poor devil to Coventry.
- *Ego needs*:   Aha, we are what we are – and this next rung on Maslow's ladder is concerned with our widely varying but innate needs for status, recognition and, in general, the respect of our fellows – both in and out of work.
- *Self-fulfilment needs*:   The top of the tree – the needs to realize one's own potential (whatever that may be) to be creative in one way or another, to become the fully self-fulfilled person one knows one is capable of being.

So, with all this in mind, I hope you will appreciate the importance of Question 12 – and the message exemplified by the proffered alternatives. The Entwhistles of this world bring their unsatisfied needs to work and it pays handsome dividends to have in-depth knowledge of approximately where each subordinate is squatting on Maslow's ladder at any given point in time. For, remember, if you want good performance *and* satisfied workers (and you should) you'll only achieve this marvellous dual objective by providing the help and means for the satisfaction of their very human needs.

Question 13

Inside knowledge of the extent to which individual subordinates are actively involved in hobbies and other leisure activities is of importance to the thinking manager, for this will help him to establish which of his juniors are blessed with that very desirable quality, fire in the belly; which, let's face it, is an essential prerequisite when it comes to allocating additional responsibilities, presenting challenges, highlighting potential promotees and so on. But, *caveat emptor*, when considering and weighing what your people do with themselves in their spare time, don't fall into the trap of viewing their chosen interests and activities through the fly-blown screen of your own prejudices, will you? Just because you're a kidney-bashing road jogger and bodybuilder in your spare time, it doesn't follow that Entwhistle's preference for stamp collecting marks him down as a complete wet.

Question 14
The ultra-ticklish area of marital and other relationships – you don't need me to tell you that this is where those flapping ears and searchlight eyes come into their own. Despite all the well-meaning gubbins about employees voluntarily seeking the advice of their managers on personal problems, it's more than likely that Joe won't come clean with this kind of trouble until it's reached roaring crisis proportions. Remember, at the very least, forearmed is forewarned.

Questions 15 and 16
What more can I say – other than to urge that you need to know exactly what troubles, if any, are threatening the quality and stability of performance of anyone within your charge.

THE DREADED BLACKLIST OF BAD PERFORMERS

Despite all our efforts at employee selection (of which enough said) and despite all our efforts to manage our people fairly and well, it seems that we're well-nigh fated to end up saddled with an unfair proportion of scalleywags, miscreants and oddballs in our respective teams. For convenience, one can plonk these undesirables into three broad categories; namely:

- Those who are middling to downright poor performers,
- Those who break the rules,
- Those who sport quite definite, difficult-to-live-with quirks of personality.

First, a word on the poor performer. Let's get a little bit personal and imagine that you are faced with just such an employee. Painful though it may be, it's worth remembering that someone, if not your blessed self, recruited the poor performer in the first place and, by so doing, rubber-stamped an authoritative decision to the effect that the person concerned was fit in every reasonable respect for the vacancy. Unhappily, the employee's subsequent poor performance serves to confirm that this original management decision was ill-founded and erroneous. Therefore, by all that's holy, it's down to you to remember this grievous error of judgement and that does *not* mean sacking the guy or gal out of hand. Every effort must be made to train the employee up to the required standard – and that means more than one crack of the training whip, adequate periods of time in which to demonstrate an improvement and a fair system of warnings.

What we need to do now is pay heed to some disciplinary ground rules, noting that they apply equally to poor performers and disciplinary offenders:

1   Apropos of disciplinary policies and procedures, it should be the case (and, hopefully, is) that your firm has all this important stuff set out in black and white. If so, examine the ordained procedure with care and compare the validity of its various requirements with those set out (in the UK) in the Advisory, Conciliation and Arbitration Service's code of practice *Disciplinary Practice and Procedures in Employment*, obtainable from ACAS or Her Majesty's Stationery Office. If your firm lacks a published disciplinary procedure – well, it's very much in your interest to ensure that they pull their finger out and produce one, using the ACAS code of practice as a guide.

2   Always remember that in the world of employment, dismissal is the capital punishment. Far too many managers treat it lightly – until, of course, it happens to them. When considering the dismissal of an employee, ask yourself the one, big question:

IN THE LIGHT OF *ALL* THE CIRCUMSTANCES AND CASTING ASIDE ALL EMOTIVE THOUGHT, WOULD A DECISION TO DISMISS BE THE ACTION OF A *REASONABLE* EMPLOYER?

3   Never allow an employee to demonstrate continued poor

performance or commit a string of minor offences without taking formal action. To do otherwise is to kick one's reputation and disciplinary policy straight into touch. By the way, my use of the phrase 'formal action' does not necessarily mean that I am advocating the business of 'formal warnings' but, rather, that you should do something positive.

4 Always conduct your disciplinary investigations and hearings with scrupulous attention to detail and in strict accordance with the natural laws of justice – remembering that one such requirement is that justice should be *seen* to be done. Remember that Sword of Damocles – the industrial tribunal.

And now we come to my third category of undesirables, the ubiquitous odd-balls and 'personality baddies' – of which there's a legion. Let me cast the limelight of recognition on just a few of them.

The saboteur

No, not the villain who sets out to plant a stick of gelignite in the executive loo – the creature I have in mind is far more insidious than that. I'm referring to the wretched individual who, whatever you do or say, will do his level best to sabotage your efforts – and those of his colleagues. This nasty type of odd-ball will always find some way of craftily twisting or circumventing your requirements, and will take a particular delight in exploiting anyone's weaknesses to his own advantage. If you are cursed with such a subordinate, bear in mind the implied terms of any contract of employment (be it written or verbal); namely, that an employee has the duties of '*giving reasonable support*' and '*fidelity and good faith*' – so go to it!

The Goebbels-type

Cast in a slightly different mould, this employee is the propagandist of the workplace – the whisperer-in-ears, the sibilant, behind-one's-back criticizer; the purveyor of gloom and doom. Remember some other implied terms of any contract of employment, the duties of '*thoughtlessness or indiscretion*' and the requirement to refrain from '*undermining the authority of employees in supervisory or management capacities*' – and root the so-and-so out.

The assassin

Do you recall your days at school and, more to the point, the horrible boy or girl who played the role of the class sneak? Well, the workplace assassin is probably the adult version of the juvenile snitcher, in that the creature's ageing process has engendered bitterness against the human race, in general, and against his colleagues at work, in particular. This is the employee who, given the chance, will drop anyone in the proverbial, including you – and do it with consummate ease. Because they've had a lifetime of experience in knife-sticking, it's often very difficult to catch them in the act of assassination, but do try.

The infamous barrack-room lawyer

This notorious breed of employee is another example of the enemy within – difficult to nab, but dangerous, withal. Usually blessed with the gift of the gab, the barrack-room lawyer latches on to his more impressionable colleagues and spouts his legalistic claptrap in defiance of the system and anyone connected with it. Be on your guard.

MOTIVATING FOR RESULTS

It's time we attempted to draw some of our many assorted strings together and, dare I say it, come up with a recipe for success. So, I ask you to work your way through the list of ingredients in Figure 2, consider each one in relation to your situation at work, and make a solemn promise to yourself that, from now until the day of your happy retirement from the fray, you'll cook this management cake – *and none other*.

It only remains to ask – have you got all that?

WORKBOX NUMBER 3

Teaser 1

Imagine (if it's not already a fact) that your organization is

**You as a leader
are responsible
for**

> *Recognizing, catering for and managing the*
> **group needs** *of your people, by:*

- Encouraging joint objective-setting
- Fostering a common sense of purpose
- Engendering a group identity
- Creating team incentives

> *Recognizing, catering for and managing the*
> **individual needs** *of your people by*

- Maximizing your knowledge of each person's background, character, fears and aspirations
- Identifying, utilizing and stretching (not straining) all personal abilities
- Demonstrating understanding, empathy and faith in each individual
- Being consistently firm but fair in your disciplinary approach

> *Managing the* **group tasks** *by:*

- Ensuring that you *plan, organize, delegate* and *control* efficiently
- Fairly *monitoring* and *evaluating* results, giving help and advice where necessary, and praise where due

*But you will only meet with success in
discharging these onerous responsibilities
if you adopt*

A consultative/participative management style

Figure 2

being buffeted by the winds of enforced change. Your particular market is rapidly becoming more competitive and, if the company is to maintain any degree of success, it is crystal-clear that, among many other things, the directors' somewhat autocratic style of management which has been practised for years must be ditched in favour of a more enlightened approach. Fortunately, the way has been paved for just such a change by the appointment of a new MD, who made it quite plain at his first monthly meeting that, like it or not, his executives were to rethink their responsibilities in terms of adopting a more open, participative-cum-consultative style of management.

As Production Manager (or whatever you choose to style yourself) you welcomed this mini-bombshell, because you've felt for a very long time that certain of your colleagues were their own worst enemies in terms of effectively managing their subordinates. As luck would have it, your enthusiasm was obviously apparent to the MD who, forthwith, instructed you to come up with some practical ideas on how to encourage and foster a more open, participative climate.

So, having opted for your preferred management role in production, sales, administration or what-have-you, do just that.

Teaser 2
As a newly appointed manager, you plan to hold a series of general 'get-to-know-you' interviews with the individual members of your team. Plainly, you wish the exercise to be a success and, to this end, you give a deal of thought to the question of your interviewing technique. List the factors which you consider should be taken into account when conducting any type of interview.

Teaser 3
Of all the eyeball-to-eyeball interview situations, it's safe to say that most managers dislike and, in many cases, actually fear the occasion when they are required to conduct a disciplinary session. Of course, you could be the exception; in which case, I suggest that you indulge in some further candid

introspection – for, believe me, there's something wrong. However, be that as it may, there's a bit of work to be done. List what you consider to be the golden rules for conducting a disciplinary interview.

WORKBOX CRIB BANK

Teaser 1

Plainly, there are many ways by which a more open, consultative-cum-participative climate can be encouraged and fostered. Before listing some of them, I wonder if you gave some cautionary thought to the overall question of the manner in which all of us tend to resist and even fear change? Picture your (hopefully) mythical organization in this Teaser and, if you haven't already done so, remind yourself how the previously autocratically-managed workforce may well react to golden handouts of consultative-cum-participative goodies; like, for instance:

Well, now . . . (*The manager announces to his assembled flock.*) I've got you together to, er, tell you that we're going to hold, er, regular discussions on – on how things are going in general, um, work-wise. (*Pregnant silence, with the air thick with suspicion.*) Yes, er, that's the general idea – so, come on, then – who's got anything to say? (*Apart from some shuffling of feet, the silence continues.*) Look, the time's getting on. . . . You, Carruthers – what have you got to offer, eh? (*Carruthers turns slightly puce in the face and glares out of the window.*) For goodness sake, get on with it.

Seriously, you know it and I know it, a deeply encrusted management style cannot, itself, change overnight and, if we're honest, may never change until certain of its protagonists are either sacked, pensioned off or buried. Similarly, the workforce which has endured a history of autocratic management isn't likely to change *its* spots unless the change is introduced very gradually, with first-rate training in attitude-changing at the fore.

While I have no means of knowing what ideas you jotted down, here are a few for you to consider:

Training

As with the vast majority of its real-life inadequately-managed counterparts, this organization will certainly have serious problems in terms of attitudes and communication:

- Members of management are not only cursed with counter-productive, adverse attitudes – it's also well on the cards that they tend to 'work against each other' rather than think and act as a team.
- There will be sparse, if any, worthwhile communication from the top – the wholehearted application of the dreaded 'need to know' principle.
- As a consequence, there'll be damn-all in the way of useful upward communication – thereby putting the seal on a gale-force 'them and us' situation.
- Departmental antagonism and jealousies will be rife.
- Individual members of the workforce will suffer dis-interest, disillusionment and fear – thus bolstering the overall problems of low morale, poor quality of work and output.

As I have already implied, all these ailments (and more) can only be corrected by sound and effective training.

Participative ventures

The main objective is not only to get people talking together, but *sharing* notions, views and headaches – and a right-minded management will do their level best to achieve this objective by; for example:

- Holding fairly regular, informal meetings of *all* members of the management team, *including* those absolutely vital, front-line managers, the supervisors, foremen and chargehands.
- Instituting quality circles in *all* departments, thereby permitting and encouraging the free and participative flow of ideas. Management will also demonstrate faith in these founts of likely wisdom by *following up all worthwhile proposals to their logical conclusion.*
- Implementing a programme of departmental (and inter-

departmental) brainstorming sessions, preferably con-
ducted away from the company, for all the managers and
supervisors concerned. Take my word for it, it's quite
amazing how the one topic, 'What are our problems;
where are we going and how do we get there?', can
produce spectacular results at such sessions.

• Creating a career development programme for all employees – if only to the extent of identifying and utilizing
hitherto unrecognized abilities and talents.

• Ensuring that delegation is implemented wisely and well
– and, yes, this could mean some more training.

• Ensuring that *all* employees know exactly how and where
they fit into the company scheme of things; where what
they make or help to make goes, and what it does; how
each and every function throughout the company makes
an important contribution to the endeavour, as a whole.

Think about these and your notions – and get cracking!

Teaser 2

These are the factors I have in mind:

1 *The aim of the interview*:   Why is it being held? What is the
desired outcome? What is one prepared to accept?

2 *Preparation*:   Have available and study all the relevant
information on the interviewee before the session takes
place.

3 *Timing of the brute*:   Is it the best time? How long will it
run – and, allowing for a moderate 'overrun', has
sufficient time been allocated to the session?

4 *Interruptions*:   Conduct the session within a 'closed
office'; post a warning notice on the door and cancel all
telephone calls.

5 *Communication*:   Listen with care – reflect empathy and
understanding. Show a *genuine* interest in all that is said.
Remember that an interview should be a steered discussion and, with the possible exception of the most
serious of disciplinary sessions, a *friendly*, steered
discussion.

6 *Courtesy*:   It costs nothing and is vital to the successful

outcome of any human transaction, let alone the interview.

Teaser 3
Little wonder that we dislike and even fear disciplinary
sessions, for they require very careful handling. Here are my
suggested golden rules for comparison with your list:

- Always keep calm and relaxed. Avoid adopting po-stances,
  po-expressions and po-gestures like the plague.
- Always annunciate the offence or fall-down in clear and
  unemotional terms.
- Listen to, and visibly consider, all explanations.
- If relevant, always explain in detail what must be done to
  rectify the slip and give a reasonable deadline for the
  required improvement.
- If a punishment is involved, explain this in concise detail,
  but do not launch into a harangue – for once sentence has
  been pronounced, the court is over. The disciplinary
  interviewer should never regard himself as a paid-up
  member of the Spanish Inquisition – or Judge Jeffries, for
  that matter.

How did you do? I'll say this, friend – by golly, you're a
sticker.

4 It's the job that counts

ENSURING THAT THE JOBS ARE RIGHT – AND STAY RIGHT

It is possible (but you won't catch me betting on it) that I can spare you much of this chapter by the simple expedient of posing one question; namely:

> Are all your people in possession of adequately detailed, up-to-date job descriptions?

Hum, well, it's likely that your reply will take one of the following forms:

Of course, they've got job descriptions – and, yes, they're all entirely adequate and up-to-date, too.

(*In which outstanding case, congratulations, thou good and faithful manager – please feel free to draw a veil over lots in this chapter of what, to you, will be second-hand stuff.*)

Er, yes – they've all got job descriptions. I know they have, because it was only three or four years ago when I had that shindig with the union over getting the wretched things drawn up.

I think they've all got them – bar the latest newcomers, that is. As for being up-to-date, I'm a bit uncertain on that point.

(*Sorry, but responses along these lines fail on a technicality – read on, my friend.*)

No, I'm afraid my people haven't got job descriptions.

Job descriptions, you say? They're a complete waste of time.

What are job descriptions, like?

(There will now be a short silence while, strictly under my breath, I throw epithets in your direction. . . . Now read on.)

There is absolutely no excuse for any manager worthy of the name who (a) fails to produce written job descriptions for each and every one of his subordinates, and (b) fails to ensure that these vital documents are regularly discussed with the employees concerned and up-dated when necessary. And just in case you are about to burst into flame, let me lay it firmly on the line.

Some artful wretches of managers go out of their way to avoid defining subordinates' jobs – usually because they fondly believe that anyone in possession of a job description will then refuse to do anything which is not engraved on the paper in letters a foot high. Of course, another reason for ducking out of the task is sheer laziness – isn't it? Either way, it's an indication of downright slipshod management. Among other things, adequate job descriptions are well-nigh invaluable prerequisites to efficient selection and job evaluation and can be a great help in resolving conflicting views on the nature and content of individuals' jobs. So, for goodness sake, let's agree on their vitality and examine just how one should set about acquiring them.

FIRST COMES THE JOB ANALYSIS

No, don't scamper for the cupboard under the stairs – job analysis isn't half as bad as it's sometimes painted. Think about it, any job consists of a series of tasks; some of them major, some minor, but all are part and parcel of the job as a whole. Job analysis is merely the process of identifying these component tasks and systematically recording (preferably, in discussion with the jobholder) and facts about each one:

1 Pinpoint each task (each separate work activity).
2 Describe the procedures involved in each task.
3 Delineate the jobholder's responsibilities associated with each task.
4 List the personal abilities, qualities, qualifications and experience required of the jobholder in respect of each task.

All right, carrying out a job analysis is clearly no sinecure, but neither is the task of management, as a whole – so get to it! Remember, the manager who completes this exercise holds the key to accurate job descriptions in his hot little hand.

AND NOW WE COME TO IT – THE JOB DESCRIPTION, ITSELF

We're getting there. The job description is a formal document which, again and wherever possible, should be drawn up in discussion with the individual concerned. Basically, it should take the following form:

- *Job identification*:   These details should include the job title and the department or section concerned.
- *The purpose of the job*:   This should comprise a concise statement of the major objectives of the job.
- *The duties of the job*:   This section should list all the tasks which have been identified in the job analysis.
- *The responsibilities of the job*:   Similarly, this section should list all the responsibilities identified in the job analysis.
- *Relationships*:   First, this section should highlight the job title of the person to whom the employee is directly responsible. Then, all other relevant working relationships (within and without the organization) should be listed.
- *Conditions of work*:   This section should detail the hours of work involved, overtime and unsocial hours, if applicable, together with reference to any particularly 'adverse' working conditions involved – a dirty or noisy environment, etc.
- *Remuneration*:   This section should comprise full details of the pay for the job, together with any related 'perks' or fringe benefits.

Since teacher wouldn't dream of asking you to do something he wouldn't do himself, what follows is an example of a typical job description. Mull it over and ensure that *your* efforts are better in every respect.

Job description

Job title: Assistant Sewage Effluent Operative Grade II

Department: Domestic Service

Purpose

Working in conjunction with nominated team members, to assist in the remedy/repair of domestic sewage effluent blockages, seepages, leakages, floods and nauseous or contaminating efflusions arising from such defects.

Duties

1   To assist in the assembly and use of all rodding equipment, including rubber pistons (large, medium and small), solid waste corkscrew extractors, steel prodders and saw-toothed gnurlers.

2   To wash down and clean all the items of equipment named in 1, above, before reloading in the company vehicle.

3   When so directed by the Sewage Effluent Team Supervisor, to take up position within a manhole or other available orifice downstream of any blockage and deliver a clear verbal report when it is evident that such blockage has been cleared.

4   In instances involving large-bore domestic out-falls, and when so directed by the Sewage Effluent Team Supervisor, to penetrate the outfall concerned and, using the bucket and spade provided for the purpose, clear the outfall of blockages.

Responsibilities

In conjunction with other members of the team, to ensure that rigorous standards of safety and cleanliness are practised and maintained during all operations on domestic premises, particularly in relation to the inadvertent fouling of customers' property or persons.

Relationships

To report directly to the Sewage Effluent Team Supervisor.

Conditions of work

The hours of work are 6.30 a.m. to 9.30 p.m., Mondays to

Sundays, inclusive. Overtime is payable for all duly authorized periods of work exceeding two hours in duration, when such overtime pay shall commence at the expiry of the second hour. In view of the nature of the work, the company supplies suitable protective clothing (e.g., plimsolls, smock overall, rubber gloves), to be regularly cleaned at the employee's expense.

Remuneration

The employee is hourly-paid at the rate of £1.00 per hour, payable three-weekly in arrears at cease-work on applicable Mondays. Overtime pay at the basic rate × 0.85 will be paid as soon as is practicable after the period of overtime concerned. The employee is entitled to membership of the company's private medical scheme on payment of the subscription charges currently in force. The employee is also permitted to remove a reasonable quantity of solid/semi-solid effluent from any work site for use as garden fertilizer, provided that the employee uses his own receptacle and arranges transport of the material at his own expense.

FOR THE SELECTION-KEEN – THE EMPLOYEE SPECIFICATION

In selection, the job description is used in conjunction with another formal document, the employee specification – which could be described with some accuracy as the 'blueprint' of the ideal candidate. The square–one starting point for writing an employee specification is a brief description of the primary duties of the job, followed by details of the age range and other particular requirements relevant to the position and, finally, a list of the main abilities sought; set out as in the following example:

Ability	Essential	Desirable
Skill in delivering instruction in the given subject areas	At least two years' previous instructing experience in the given subject areas	Full or Associate Membership of the Institute of Training and Development

THE NITTY-GRITTY BUSINESS OF JOB EVALUATION

Sooner or later (and the Great God Nemesis usually ensures that it's sooner rather than later), nearly every manager comes eyeball-to-eyeball with the dreaded task of job evaluation – dreaded because it ranks high on the list of processes which, unless one is very careful, will provoke a right old shindig among the employees concerned. So, grabbing our courage with both hands, let's take a gentle romp through the various methods of attaching a value, finally expressed in terms of lollie, to this or that group of jobs.

Job ranking

This method of job evaluation is the tried-and-awful approach utilized by the uninformed majority in our midst. Quite simply (using the term advisedly, everything about the process can be said to be simple) it entails looking at all the jobs concerned and, by fair means or foul, arranging them in relative order of value by 'ranking' one job against another. Thus it may well be that Bertie Manager will evaluate, say, a secretary's job along the following lines of deep and magnificent thought:

> Aha, now let me see – I've got to evaluate this new slot of secretary to the Admin Manager. . . . Um, well, the MD's secretary is screwing us for £x, don't know how the old fool ever agreed to that – and young Lisa, the secretary in Sales is getting £y. Then, there's Maggie over in Production – she's drawing £z. . . . How the hell does all that help me? I'll try another tack. . . . Which is the most important secretarial post? Huh, I know what I think, but that doesn't count for anything round here – it has to be the MD's creature. Who comes next – Sales, Production or this new job? I suppose one way of looking at it is, er, well, whenever I see Maggie, she's always bashing away at something or other – whereas, for my money, that girl Lisa spends most of her time making eyes at the sales reps. . . . Cripes, which one really does

the most work, I wonder? There's one thing for sure, I'd better err on the safe side, or there'll be hell to play.

And so on and so forth.

In sum, job ranking can be, and usually is, a very subjective, hit-or-miss method of job evaluation.

Points rating

This method entails attaching a points value to the various factors which, in sum, comprise each of the jobs under review. For example, it may be decided that factors such as knowledge, skills, experience, the extent of resources controlled, levels of authority, etc. are identified as most relevant in assessing the comparative value of the jobs concerned. Each factor is then allotted a range of points so that a maximum number of points is available; say:

		Total possible points available
Knowledge		60
Skills: Mental	30	
Physical	30	60
Experience		60
Resources controlled		50
Effort required		40
Adverse job conditions		50

Then comes the difficult bit. The comparative value of the factors in each job is determined i.e., the factor of 'knowledge' in Job A may be allocated a 'score' of 30 out of the possible total of 60, while the same factor in Job B, which we'll assume is a far more complex post requiring extensive knowledge, may be allocated 60 points. Next, the total of the factor scores for each job is totted up to produce the final points evaluation in each case – and then they are ranked in order of score. Finally, if the determination of pay rates is the object of the exercise, monetary values will be attached to the various scores – often by clumping together 'batches' of scores into pay grades.

Job classification

This method of job evaluation is somewhat similar to the job ranking approach, in that the jobs are still regarded as complete entities. However, in job classification, the initial move is to establish a number of pay grades and then allocate a single 'key' or 'benchmark' job to each grade. Every other job is then examined to ascertain which key job it is closest to and, ergo, it is allocated to the relevant pay grade. As you'll doubtless appreciate, job classification can be carried out fairly quickly but, as with job ranking, the results are pretty well bound to be highly subjective.

For this man's money, the task of job evaluation is best carried out by the points rating method which, while it's still a subjective process, is a jolly sight less so than the others.

A SHORT PAUSE FOR REFLECTION

Thus far, we've considered job analysis, job descriptions, employee specifications and job evaluation and, since I'm obviously advocating that you should put what I preach into effective practice, I'm forced to acknowledge that, to some of us, there's a fairly strong disincentive so to do. There's a good deal of work involved – all of it 'non-productive' in that, with the exception of the employee in personnel, it could be said to have precious little relevance to any manager's primary, profit-making function. To make things worse, much of this slog consists of paperwork, and we all know how Jack and Jill at the sharp end of management will generally move mountains in order to avoid any form of lengthy and laborious written stuff.

But, reader, you're the one who was sufficiently interested to beg, borrow, steal or (praise be) buy this book, and if you still wish to improve your effectiveness as a people-manager, then grasp the flaming nettle! Did I say it was going to be easy?

It's time to pose another question.

TO WHAT EXTENT DO YOU EFFECTIVELY MANAGE YOUR PEOPLE IN TERMS OF TRAINING?

Dear me, if past experience is anything to go by, we've put

our finger on yet another topic that, given half a chance, could plummet to the floor like a lump of wet dough. However, the evidence is that, at long last, there's a wind of change (more like a zephyr of breeze, actually) where our national attitude to training is concerned. So, instead of launching into the well-worn sermon, I'll simply assume that you are 'training-conscious' and invite you to join me in an examination of how best to improve your existing know-how. And, lest we forget it, your people's know-how.

THE ALL-IMPORTANT IDENTIFICATION OF TRAINING NEEDS

Let's first illustrate the process of identifying training needs by resorting to the type of sum that even I can understand:

KNOWLEDGE AND SKILLS REQUIRED *minus* PRESENT KNOWLEDGE AND SKILLS *equals* A TRAINING NEED

Remember the job description? Provided it's accurate, it is this document that'll furnish us with details of all the tasks that comprise an employee's job. So, if we use this list as a starting-point, we can annotate each task with the *required levels of skill and knowledge* relevant to it; for example:

Task	Knowledge required	Skills required
Operation and maintenance of petty cash account	Cash book entry and balancing procedures, familiarity with procedures and documentation for cash advances and reimbursements	Ability to undertake simple calculations, ability to handle cash

Once we have established the 'total' required levels of knowledge and skill in respect of all the jobs under review, we can proceed to identify the *present* levels of knowledge and skill possessed by each of the job holders, and thus determine individual deficiencies – the training needs of the people concerned. Admittedly, this business of establishing an accurate picture of existing levels of knowledge and skill is easier said than done. If an appraisal scheme is in operation (and *if* the information thus provided is not wildly subjective) this part of the analysis should be quite straightforward. If not, or if the scheme is not worth the paper it's printed on, then one is down to the nitty-gritty of performance and production inspection, and in-depth discussion with each of the people involved.

THE PLANNING STAGE

If you have a fair number of subordinates, it's likely that you will end up with a mini-stack of individual training needs littering your desk. So, like the good manager you are, you'll create order out of chaos by drawing up an overall training plan. The actual order of training play will certainly be influenced by the money available in the budget (but do remember such possible goodies as government training grants), the times when personnel can be spared from their duties and, if you're wise, the all-vital question of priorities.

Apropos training, and because I always believe in looking on the blackest side of any picture, I've assumed up to now that your organization isn't blessed with the presence of a training officer-cum-manager. If you do have such a valuable person on the pay roll, all well and good, but don't run away with the idea that this lets you off the hook. It's still down to you as a responsible manager to carry out your training needs analysis, albeit with some professional help, lay your plans and then check out the whole caboodle with the trainer.

Let's continue on the assumption that, like it or not, you're on your jolly own.

DON'T BE LED LIKE AN EXECUTIVE-LAMB TO THE SLAUGHTER

One only has to flick through any professional or trade journal to realize that the training world is chock-a-block with eager beavers who, in return for large lumps of money, will be only too happy to train your people in anything under the sun. Unfortunately, many of them are cowboys. So, if it's necessary for you to look outside your organization for the odd course or seminar, take care to consult everyone and everybody before parting with a brass farthing; such as:

● Your local college of further education.
● The area office of the Training Commission.
● Any group training association within convenient reach. Many of these excellent bodies are willing to open their doors to non-member companies and individuals, if only on an initial 'sampling' basis.
● If you have one, your Industry Training Board.
● Pop along to your local library and get them to fish out a copy of the latest *Personnel and Training Yearbook*, published by Kogan Page. You should find this publication of great help.

TELL ME, HAVE YOU THOUGHT OF OPEN LEARNING?

You shouldn't need me to remind you that training for business and industry in this competitive age has to be practical, flexible and cost-effective. Open Learning achieves all these aims by developing people without taking them away from their work for those all-too-expensive, long periods of time. It offers opportunities for distance learning in a whole mass of subjects and topics – telephone, video and tape cassette tuition, face-to-face tutorials, drop-in study facilities, inter-personal skills workshops and so on. Plainly, the Open College or any of the reference sources I've already mentioned should be your targets for further inquiries.

TRAINING EVALUATION – THE ESSENTIAL AFTERMATH

Turn your memory back to the last time you underwent some training at your employer's behest, and ask yourself to what extent your boss interested himself in finding out whether you had achieved any specific improvements in your performance as a result of the training? The likelihood is that on your return to the galley you were asked if the course 'had been any good' – capped, I don't wonder, with a slightly pithy reminder that your beanfeast was over and that it only remained for you to come down from the clouds and get on with some work. A slightly cynical observation, do you think? No, me hearty, par for the course!

Training is a damned expensive investment and, to put it bluntly, it's money down the drain if you fail to question exactly how far it has achieved its purpose. Yes, evaluation is difficult, but it has to be done.

All right, one has to seek reactions from trainees. In other words, the good old question, 'How did it go?', has to be asked. But, for goodness sake, don't just leave it at that – find out from the people concerned how interesting (and, yes, how enjoyable) the training was. Ascertain their detailed views of the various sessions, whether or not these were relevant to individual training needs, and what they thought of the speakers involved. Such an exercise will provide you with good, solid information and, incidentally, will do much to improve your stature in their eyes as a manager who is interested in their welfare and progress.

Check, as far as is possible, the 'training yield' in terms of learning and subsequent behaviour. Have the newly trained lads and lassies actually learned what they should have learned and, just as important, to what extent and *how* are they applying these golden nuggets of knowledge to their work?

In sum, training is all about improving performance, but is that the end of the story? Do we just want to convert our juniors into super-effective, automaton-like work units – or is there something else? You bet your sweet life there is!

IT'S CALLED JOB ENRICHMENT

The other week, I listened with my usual avid curiosity to a manager-chappie who was talking about the general set-up within his particular bailiwick at work. As a production manager, he is (at least, I hope he still is) responsible, among other things, for some twenty operatives who are engaged in the assembly of electronic gizmos for the aerospace industry – jobs which he agreed are intensely repetitive and boring. Much to my surprise, he admitted on polite questioning that not one of these twenty-odd women had more than a vague idea of the ultimate function and use of the things they were making and then went on to assert that 'with their attitude to work, it would be a waste of time telling them anyway'.

It was at that point that I kind of fell out with the manager concerned, for nothing infuriates me more than this type of slipshod disregard for the fact that employees, whatever their status, are human beings, not work units, and should always be treated as such. To me (and, if you so wish, you can call me impractically idealistic until you're blue in the face because I know I'm right), the minutes-long act of telling such employees the full purpose and destiny of whatever their boredom-chained efforts produce will, at the very least, create an iota of motivation in some of them, and that makes the exercise more than worthwhile.

I guess we'd better start with a definition of what job enrichment is all about and, in my view, there's none better than the down-to-earth statement that it ignites and fans the flames of interest and challenge of work – almost any work. Here are some of the techniques by which this most laudable aim can be achieved:

1 First, and as I've already indicated, by telling your people as much as is possible about the 'end-product' of their work – the *what*, *why*, *where* and *how* components, if you like.

2 By providing them with opportunities to vary and personally improve their work methods and processes.

3 In production, by so arranging the team tasks that individual members or groups of employees can produce as near a 'whole' unit as possible.

4 By training workers to carry out their own checks for quality control, rather than have the whole lot imposed on them by the QC section.

5 By allowing them to participate in planning work, seeking innovation, setting targets and standards of performance.

6   By increasing personal responsibilities, in general.

7   By setting up quality circles (of which more anon), and ensuring that sound proposals arising from them receive full and visible consideration – in other words, not just the usual lip service.

8   By assigning individual employees or groups specific projects, thereby stretching their abilities and providing an element of that good old gut-stirrer, challenge in their work.

9   And last but not least, by initiating your job enrichment programme with a get-together of all concerned, to seek *their* views and proposals. After all, who knows most about work at the sharp end and its problems? Why, *they* do.

The benefits provided by sensibly applied job enrichment have to be seen to be believed – so go to it.

A FEW THOUGHTS ON PAY

It could be said that any worthwhile payment system should embrace a number of significant objectives; namely:

1   First and foremost (and so often the heap-big stumbling-block), to enable an employee to earn good and reasonable money.

2   To provide a realistically fair reward for high levels of performance and output.

3   To provide equitable remuneration across-the-board and, for some diehard employers in this country, that includes getting round to observing the provisions of the Equal Pay Act 1970.

4   To provide an incentive for people to use their own initiative.

5   To be easily understandable by those who have to endure it.

While it may well be that you don't have the direct authority (or, I'd better add, financial capability – even though that is open to debate) to do anything much about items 1, 2 and 3 above, this does not excuse you from one of the primary responsibilities of a manager – that is, to push *and push hard* for any improvements at work where improvements are clearly necessary. To some, this means that, come what may, fears of Big Daddy, losing one's job and being labelled a 'Red' have to be squashed underfoot – so, if this cap fits, grow up and earn *your* money. Present a logical and compelling argument for change for the better, and stand by it. In general, examine your pay structures in depth and find out exactly whether or not they meet the five objectives – and, if not, trot into well-planned action. Consider the various methods of remuneration:

- Fixed salaries with regular reviews.
- Fixed salaries with irregular reviews.
- Incremental salaries.
- Individual piecework or payment-by-results.
- Group piecework.
- Standard time systems.
- Indirect labour bonus schemes.
- Total factory/company bonus schemes.
- Measured day work.
- Productivity bargaining.
- Profit sharing.

While the above list is by no means exhaustive, it may serve as food for thought where the pay structure for your people is concerned. Is it a fair and equitable system? Is it simple to understand and operate, or is it so illogical and complicated that it defies description? Even if, on close inspection, you can find nothing much wrong, get thee to a library and mug up on pay systems, in general – for the odds are that your particular pay structure could well be improved. For instance, if it is specifically intended to reward and encourage employees to produce high levels of *output* rather than (as is often the case) *high-quality work*, it could be that a pay structure based on some type of piecework system would be more appropriate – and vice versa.

SUGGESTION SCHEMES

Suggestion schemes are like some seedlings – plant them in the wrong soil and they either go berserk or simply wither away. A typical scenario is the outfit in which employee relations are at an all-time low, and the management team is frantically trying to dream up remedies which (a) won't cost them any money, and (b) will involve them in minimal effort:

> Aha, I know what we'll do. . . . (*Says the manager.*) Let's start a suggestion scheme – what do you think of that for an idea, eh? (*Blank looks from his assembled management minions.*) Look, we've got to do something, right? (*Manager glares round the table.*) So, George, you knock up some boxes and place them round the factory and I'll issue a notice telling everyone that any suggestions for, er, well, improving production and what-not will be considered by . . . : suppose it had better be me. (*Silence prevails, broken only by the accountant who is cracking his knuckles with agitation.*) Yes, I think that's a splendid idea – it'll probably do wonders to raise morale, and we could shell out the odd fiver for really first-rate suggestions. . . . Any questions? No? Right, that's that settled, then.

In such situations, it doesn't require all that much imagination to picture the outcome of the manager's inspired idea. In no time flat, the suggestion boxes are crammed with toffee papers, old fag packets and discarded oil-rags – together, it must be admitted, with a number of hastily scrawled, anonymous proposals on what the management can do with their suggestion scheme. The moral to this cautionary illustration is obvious; do anything rather than impose a suggestion scheme, however marvellous, on a discontented workforce – for the result will always be embarrassingly painful.

On the other hand, if the organization climate is sufficiently balmy to nurture the acceptance and use of a suggestion scheme – why, then proceed with due caution:

1   Ensure that the proposed scheme embraces all departments within the outfit, not just a chosen one or two.
2   Don't resort to suggestion boxes – have them forward their suggestions to nominated people.

3   Set up (and announce) that a committee with manager reps
    from all departments will consider all suggestions.
4   Publicize that all viable, 'winning' suggestions will attract
    a worthwhile, *initial* cash award and that those which are
    subsequently found to produce significant savings to the
    company will entitle the originators to further, pre-
    determined 'percentage' awards.
5   Provided the originators agree, make a suitable song and
    dance about winning suggestions.
6   Acknowledge the receipt of all suggestions and, after
    consideration, write a suitable note of thanks to those who
    didn't win an award.
7   Pay up as promised – promptly!

   I think it's high time that I made a suggestion. If you really
wish to ensure that your juniors' jobs are all hunky-dory and
that they're deriving maximum satisfaction from that which
they do, then pay constant attention, not lip service, to the
one-and-only creed – *it's the job that counts.*

WORKBOX NUMBER 4

Teaser 1
While one of my aims in this chapter was to prod you into
thinking about and using job descriptions, I'm a bit of a realist.
I know as well as the next man that, if you're cast in a certain
mould, you'll have read the words and, using whatever excuse
came handily to mind, ignored them. Given this type of
head-in-sand approach, I also realize that you'll be scanning
these lines with exactly the same detached laziness. However,
if nothing else, I'm a tryer and here's a last-ditch attempt on
my part to bring you to your management senses.
   First, if you're not already in possession of a fairly adequate,
up-to-date job description, get onto your boss at the earliest
opportunity and convince His Holiness that you damned well
should have one. It's possible that he'll counter your well-
aimed brickbat by instructing you to analyse your job and
compose a draft job description for his approval, which, in
fact, is quite a good thing. But, come what may, get yourself
one, right?

Second, in the event that you have failed to supply your juniors with job descriptions, now is the time to extract *your* mismanaging digit and set the ball rolling to equip each person with what is rightfully theirs. Yes, it's a job of work but, reader, *if you can't stand the heat, get out of the kitchen.*

Teaser 2
Think training and, having got your mind into gear, produce some form of '*training achieved*' chart in respect of all the members of your team. Aim at producing something along the lines of the chart in Figure 3.

	Training achieved			
Name	*Date* 28 APR 88	*Date* 1-5 JUN 88	*Date*	
BLOGGS, J.	*Subject* B.W. T'MISSIONS	*Subject* AUTOTUNE DIAG. EQUIP.	*Subject*	
	Date 11-15 AUG 88	*Date*	*Date*	
CRUMP, P.	*Subject* WARRANTY CLAIMS	*Subject*	*Subject*	

Figure 3

Of course, when completed, it could be that your chart represents nothing more than a series of blank spaces, which must mean something in terms of getting to grips with a training plan. But do it, anyway.

Teaser 3
Teaser 1 was plainly directed at the scalleywag-reader. Who knows, if you're a manager who does possess a job description and who has ensured that all his people have them too, why, you'll have sailed through that little bit with a lily-white conscience and absolutely nothing to do.

I hate to say this, but now it's your turn. Announce to your team that you are going to review their existing job descriptions, allot each of them an interview appointment and ask them to attend their respective sessions armed with constructive comments and proposals, if any, for change. It might also be a good idea to take the opportunities offered by the interviews to explore questions of future training and development with each individual.

WORKBOX CRIB BANK

Teasers 1 and 3
Oh, no – you're on your own!

Teaser 2
Think training – and as a further step along the way, consider implementing a realistic programme for the systematic training of your people:

1 Identify their individual training needs.
2 Define the training objectives in terms of realistic, *measurable* goals.
3 Prepare the training plan – defining the overall scheme, types and methods of training, costs and benefits.
4 Define the methods of measuring and analysing the results.
5 Determine how feedback (the validation of the training) is to be ensured.

If, like me, you're a devil for expressing everything in diagrammatic form (and I cannot think of a better way to highlight the relationships between the component parts of any system) Figure 4 shows the application of systematic training.

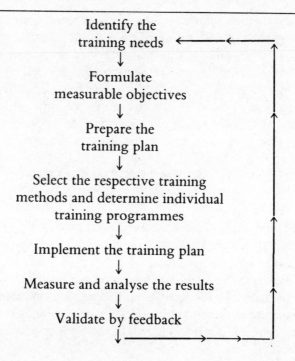

Figure 4

5   Garbage in – and, yes, garbage out

MAKING ONE'S REQUIREMENTS KNOWN – AND GETTING RESULTS

While I don't think I believe in fairies at the bottom of one's garden and all that jazz, I'm completely unashamed to admit that I have a most profound belief in *gremlins*. In fact, as I sit keying this stuff into my word processor, I know beyond a shadow of doubt that at least a platoon of the little horrors have me in their sights – gleefully determined, as ever, to get me where it hurts and wreak havoc with whatever I'm doing. Now, it may well be that you, reader, are a pure-at-heart innocent who doesn't share my belief; so, please, let me set you right.

Gremlins are invisible, malicious little demons whose purpose in life is to haunt our place of work, gaily throwing bombshells left, right and centre, and, of course, when they're least expected. To make things worse, the creatures lay eggs and, in case you really are an innocent, the eggs are called *glitches*. Aha, now that we're on familiar territory, it's only necessary to add the obvious; namely, that gremlins and their glitches play merry hell with computers, machinery, secretaries, telephones and coffee-makers, infect the blood of well-intentioned managers and, above all else, foul up the human ability to communicate.

If there's something amiss with your outfit, I'm willing to lay any odds you like that poor (or rankly bad) communication is a root cause of the trouble. You know what I mean by 'root cause': it could be that Big Daddy opens his rattletrap mouth and, as a consequence, plonks an oversize hoof in the proverbial; that Annie Blenkinsop remains paralytically silent when everyone else is screaming for a decision; that old Sam Cartwright, a superannuated manager who came up the hard way, regards writing as the work of the Devil; that those bolshie-minded so-and-sos in this or that department have closed their ears to reason – or whatever. Now, lest you think from that lengthy comment that I'm preparing to launch into the well-worn, introductory lesson on communication, with all that thrilling stuff about transmitters, receivers, channel noise, feedback and so on – well, I'm not. Put it this way, if you don't already nurture and practise the basic philosophy of the art, nothing that I can write is going to change your nasty leopard's spots. So, assuming that you're at least converted to the faith, I'd ask you to kindly roll up your sleeve; for, like it or not, you're about to receive some inoculations against one form of communication thrombosis – the ever-present threat of poor-to-stinking delegation.

HOW BEST TO GET THINGS DONE

Yes, yes, yes – of course, we know that effective delegation is the very process on which the work of an organization depends. But, if we're honest, we also know that, of all our many weaknesses, our general inability to delegate wisely and well squats firmly at the head of the mighty long list. So, let's set the scene by recalling just one anonymous cry from the wilderness:

> I know you believe you understand what you think I said.
> But I'm not sure you realize that what you heard is not
> what I meant. . . .

Having taken that one little lesson to heart, I reckon it would be a good idea if we shoved the actual communication bit to one side for a minute or two; for, after all, there's precious little use in making our requirements known to our juniors if we haven't planned them in the first place. The initial, vital step must be to decide exactly *what* is to be delegated and *to whom* – and that's a process which, if we're not very careful, can plunge us head-first into a right mess of pottage.

EXAMINING THE METAPHORICAL SLOP-CHIT

Any manager's work can, and must, be regarded as falling into two essential categories – 'managing' tasks and 'operating' (or 'doing') tasks:

Managing tasks	Operating tasks
The good old functions of planning, organizing, leading, controlling, motivating, etc.	The day-to-day routine tasks which beset us all

Plainly, in terms of delegation, it is the *operating* tasks with which we are concerned and these require further subdivision:

Operating tasks

The essential tasks that require the manager's personal attention	Those tasks which are suitable for delegation

It's at this point that the wise manager will engage in a detailed examination of all the tasks which, on the surface, have been deemed to be suitable for delegation:

1 Establish the work priorities
Decide which of the tasks are:

- Priority 1, requiring immediate attention.
- Priority 2, requiring urgent but not immediate attention.
- Priority 3, constituting the remainder.

2 Establish the allocation priorities
- Priority 1 – decide which subordinate(s) is/are best qualified to undertake the tasks requiring *immediate* attention.
- Priority 2 – decide which subordinate(s) is/are best qualified to undertake the tasks requiring *urgent but not immediate* attention.
- Priority 3 – for allocation at will.

3 Carry out a final check

● Review all the tasks thus selected for delegation, and ensure their validity (remembering that many routine/ repetitive tasks tend to become obsolete), pruning where necessary.

● Examine the existing workloads of selected delegatees to ensure that they can cope with the additional tasks.

● Wherever humanly possible, confirm that the planned delegation will 'stretch' (but *not* break) the abilities of those concerned – thereby providing them with a healthy and very necessary element of challenge.

AND NOW WE'RE BACK TO THE VITAL COMMUNICATION BIT

You'll need a pencil and paper for this section – so, grabbing a cuppa on the way, beetle off to Junior's satchel or the sideboard drawer for the necessary.

Okay? Good – all you have to do is read the following miniscripts and jot down some comments on what you think of the approach to delegation revealed in each case.

Example 1
(*Production manager to his supervisor*)

Jack, we've simply got to do something about getting that batch for Germany finished by tonight . . . I know it's asking a hell of a lot, but the people upstairs have been on to me again this morning – and if we don't get them done, they'll be down on us like a ton of bricks. Be a good chap and see what you can do, will you?

Example 2
(*Old Brass-Balls to his subordinate*)

Right, understand this – I've told you all that you need to know and it's now down to you . . . I want the full draft on my desk by noon tomorrow – got it?

Example 3
(*Manager responding to subordinate's comments*)

Look, Jill, believe me, I do appreciate that what I'm asking you to do isn't really part of your job but, don't you see, here's a splendid opportunity to broaden your experience. Yes, I realize that you haven't been on the course, but you can hack it if you put your mind to it! Just get out there and pitch in – all right?

Example 4
(*Office manager addressing his chief clerk*)

See here, Jim, it's not down to you to question the whys and wherefores of every job you're given – for goodness sake, things are bad enough in the office, as it is. Just get on with it, will you?

Example 5
(*Manager to his 'old faithful' subordinate*)

Miss Wilkes, I do so hate to trouble you with this one, especially since you've got so much on your plate at present. But as a favour to me, I wonder whether you'd be good enough to. . . .

Yes, you're dead right, five examples of managers who clearly qualify for the Delegation Mug of the Month Award. Let's see how your comments compare with mine, shall we?

Example 1
There are certain mismanagers among us who find it difficult to delegate anything without (a) positively grovelling to their subordinates and (b) passing the buck by taking the name of their superiors in vain – in this case, by generic and pathetic reference to 'the people upstairs'. Such creatures should be smothered at birth.

Example 2
Old Brass-Balls is your genuine, do-it-my-way-or-else, son-of-a-gun autocrat. Suffice it to say that we've all met these

ranting, roaring horrors and, sadly, many of us have suffered under them. Effective delegation? You must be joking.

Example 3
In this example, there's more than a hint that poor Jill has protested her inability to carry out whatever is required of her, and it's also transparently clear that her wretched boss is blandishing his way through her objections. While we have relatively little to go on, there's fairly good evidence to assume that this manager is so blinded by the needs of the job that he's walking rough-shod over the needs of his subordinate, and that, my friend, is thoroughly rotten management.

Example 4
Yes, here we have more than a touch of the autocrat at work, but, equally bad, we're faced with a classic example of the manager who for reasons of impatience, or whatever, refuses to countenance any questioning of his motives (etc.) in delegating this or that task. All right, I know that the odd subordinate can drive one up the wall with a flood of inane queries and objections; but, in general and as we are to see, questions should be encouraged, not stone-walled.

Example 5
This example highlights another version of the blandisher-delegator – the type of manager who sees nothing wrong in cajoling an already overloaded subordinate to accept yet more work. We know they exist – and more's the pity.

'Pretty obvious examples,' do I hear you say? That's as may be, but they're most certainly not larger than life – I doubt that the organization exists wherein one would fail to uncover one, some or all of these delegation misfits. Why not take a long, cool look round your executive anthill and prove me wrong?

Having highlighted a few of the baddies, I reckon it's time to blow a fanfare on the proverbial trumpet and trot out the invariable four-component drill for really effective delegation. Let's emulate the Sergeant-Major and do it by numbers.

1 Instructing

When delegating all but the most trivial of tasks, there's a little more to this first step than merely spouting a flood of directions. This in itself, can present something of a daunting task to those of us who have difficulty in communicating information in a clear and logical manner. It must always follow that, having considered how best to convey the requirements of the task, *we then have to allocate the necessary authority to enable it to be carried out.*

It's at this early point in the process when umpteen managers succeed in fouling their executive nests and, lest you doubt this, consider the following, all-too-familiar complaint:

> The trouble with my boss is, he delegates this and that job but never, ever gives anyone the right amount of authority to bring them off. It's as if he's scared that he'll weaken his own flaming position or something – I tell you, it's plain exasperating at times.

It is important to remember that *authority* means *power* and that, since power is a highly explosive commodity, it should be handled like eggs. The rule must be, always give adequate authority to enable the delegate to perform the required task – in a nutshell, not too much and not too little.

2 Allocating

This second step in the four-component drill is concerned with that vital prerequisite of all delegation, *the allocation of adequate responsibility for the success or failure of the task.* The manager who requires a junior to carry out work on his behalf without clearly informing the employee of his accountability in the matter is simply bucking for trouble – so why do so many of us forget all about it?

> Remember, Joe, the 31st is the deadline.

> Let me know as soon as you've completed the check.

> Please let me have your report by Friday, at the latest.

3 Motivating

Mention the word 'motivation' to Mr Average-Manager and

it's likely that his eyes'll turn into pickled onions in a trice for, sadly, many in our ranks regard motivation as trick-cyclist stuff and, hence, strictly for the birds. But, believe me, there's pure gold in them there hills. Subordinates *must* be motivated to succeed and, in delegation, this can best be done by the simple process of putting them fully in the picture:

The main reason why I'm asking you to do this is . . .

(No, not '. . . because I don't want to do it myself', reader. The words are [or jolly well should be] the preamble to a concise and attractive explanation of why the job is necessary, what benefits will accrue and, if at all possible, why the subordinate's personal qualifications and experience will be an insurance against failure.)

At this juncture, let us also give consideration to the widely varying effects of *personal style* in delegation; i.e., the manner in which *you* make *your* requirements known. When delegating work to your people, do the actual words you use and the tones in which you utter them tend to motivate them – or do you simply frighten them or otherwise crease them up?

Do you command?
Well, put it this way, if you're not a member of the Royal Family or the Armed Services, you have no right *or* need (except in times of fire or other dire emergency) to issue commands. In business and industry, commands went out with the Ark, so don't use them – and that's an order. . . .

Do you instruct?
The likelihood is that you *do* instruct and, provided you deliver your instructions using well-chosen words delivered in a pleasant and even voice, there's every reason why you should resort to this sensible means of making your requirements known. Except, that is, when your relationship with a subordinate is such that a 'softer' approach is warranted.

Do you request?
There's a big difference between an instruction and a request, isn't there? The thinking manager who does enjoy good

relationships with his people and who *isn't* scared stiff of tumbling off his self-made pedestal will recognize the all-round advantages of the 'requesting approach' to delegation.

Or, just sometimes, do you merely suggest?
When dealing with a conscientious subordinate, the carefully-worded suggestion can work wonders – but care is obviously necessary.

Or, wretched creature, do you plead?
Make no mistake about it, the plea is the resort of the executive-slugworm. Although these spineless creatures should never be allowed within miles of a management hot seat, they're still to be found quivering like jellies in far too many organizations. But you, reader, would never dream of pleading with your subordinates, so the point is purely of academic interest, isn't it?

In sum, then, this business of motivating in delegation can be largely achieved by communicating full information to our subordinates and ensuring, overall, that we deliver this communication in meaningful, interesting and firm but pleasant terms.

4 Consulting
When delegating tasks, it's an idiot of a manager who fails to take full advantage of the undoubted wisdom and experience of those at the sharp end – the actual doers of the delegated work. Always make a point of tapping this valuable reservoir of knowledge:

Okay, Margaret, now that I've explained what's required, is there some other approach we could adopt?

Can you foresee any snags, George?

Well, John, up to now I've been doing most of the talking –what are your views? Can it be done?

And that just about rounds off this section on how best to implement delegation but, coming back to the general principles of the game, I'm afraid there's still a couple of monumental pitfalls to be considered.

CONTROLLING THE DELEGATION TAP

There are two forms of human rot which beset the delegation scene. One is the underdelegator, the manager who regards the process as something akin to the act of giving blood and, quite obviously, the other is the overdelegator, the manager who showers his hapless juniors with wholly inappropriate and undeserved work. Stand by for some home truths, and if any cap fits, be warned that not only is Nemesis standing on your tail – equally perilous, your subordinates hold you in nothing but absolute contempt.

Are you an underdelegator?

In other words, are you just plain lethargic? Only you will know if you have pure essence of indolence running in your otherwise watery bloodstream and, hence, are just too damned lazy to delegate tasks to others. If you have succumbed to this cardinal sin, there's no need to hop off your butt with worry – the Great Management Reaper will see to everything. But, tragically, in the meantime, your subordinates will continue to suffer – so don't expect them to do other than dance at your demise, will you?

Or is it the case that you're just plain insecure in your job? If you are hostage, for whatever reason, to the fear of being thrown out of your job and, as a consequence, personally hang on to every scrap of your work in a frantic attempt to appear indispensable – why, my poor deluded mismanager, you're on a hiding to nothing. Your insecurity will *show* – and no amount of withholding delegation from those who deserve and need it will prevent the final execution, if execution there's to be. So, if you do go, why not go with honour and the knowledge that, at least in one respect, you've acted in the meantime as a manager, having delegated wisely and well?

Or could it be that you simply lack confidence in your subordinates? If you know what I'm getting at, you'll be all-too-familiar with the excuses much-favoured by such pox-ridden Doubting Thomases:

With the time it takes to tell them, it's a damned sight

quicker to do the work myself.

They're just plain incompetent.

They're just not interested.

So, in the dire event that this cap fits, ask yourself a few questions. . . . Who is at fault if and when it takes ages before your instructions sink in? Who is responsible for ensuring that your people are competent at their jobs? Who is responsible for motivating them and maintaining their interest in their work? And, in very many cases, who was responsible for selecting them in the first place? *Why, you, you faithless idiot!*

Or do you have an undue concern for prestige?

Hey, look out, you deadbeats, I'm the greatest – the human dynamo, the Superman of the outfit. . . . Who cares about the subordinates, they're not sharing my kudos.

Enough said – except, perhaps, to add that this particular slope is slippery, indeed.

Or, last but not least, do you suffer from an overweening interest in the job? More often than not, workoholics are champion underdelegators and if you're one of them, it's high time that you stopped being so beastly selfish and, instead, think of handing in your chips as a self-qualified candidate for a coronary.

Are you an overdelegator?

Do you suffer from inadequate knowledge/experience? If you lack the technical expertise which is a prerequisite of your appointment, and/or you are short on general management know-how, and/or you have shortcomings in terms of personality – why, it's highly likely that you are an avid overdelegator. Only you will know and only you can correct this grievous fault.

Or, again, are you just plain lazy? This time, too damned lazy to do *anything* – except heap it all on the pain-wracked shoulders of your juniors? Well, *are you?*

Or is it that you, yourself, feel demotivated in your job? If so, is this any excuse for overworking the people under you? It isn't, and you know it.

That's about it for this chapter – I hope we're still friends.

WORKBOX NUMBER 5

Teaser 1
This little task is merely the presage of another lump of hard work, but I hope you'll accept my assurance that, once you've done all that is necessary (of which more anon) it's almost certain to pay a handsome dividend.

For the moment, consider the business of conducting a *delegation audit* with the members of your team. What do you think is the purpose of such an exercise, and what should it comprise?

Teaser 2
How can a manager's *span of control* (i.e., the number of employees who report directly to him) affect the quality of his delegation?

Teaser 3
If and when a manager encounters problems in delegating tasks to subordinates, their solution becomes a matter of urgent priority. At such times, as with all problems, the best approach is to utilize the 'six-step' problem-solving process. Have a stab at listing the six steps.

Teaser 4
Here's a simple one. What basic rules do you think should be borne in mind when allocating responsibilities and authority in delegation?

Teaser 5
What are the two main points that a manager should bear in mind when deciding whether or not a task is *suitable* for delegation?

Teaser 6
You could deem this little poser to be a mite unfair – but, it

may give you food for thought. In certain types of organization, the delegation process is implemented in an *upward* direction. Can you think of one such type of organization and briefly describe the problem commonly associated with this form of delegation?

WORKBOX CRIB BANK

Teaser 1

Yes, you're right, a delegation audit is an exercise carried out with the purpose of assessing the amount and quality of delegated work shouldered by each individual, his or her capacity for such work *and* whether or not work is being delegated to the people most suited to it.

So, now for the hard work. Find out from the members of your team exactly how they feel about the delegated work you heap (or occasionally dribble) on their individual shoulders:

- Is, in fact, the quantity too much, too little – or just right?
- Forget the width and test the quality – do individuals feel stretched *but not strained* by their delegated tasks? In other words, do you present them with tasks which represent boredom personified, decent challenges or downright ulcer-breeders?

And then place them all under the magnifying glass to determine whether or not the tasks are going to the right individuals.

Take heart, you *and* they'll feel better for it!

Teaser 2

A manager's span of control can affect the quality of his delegation because, quite simply, as the span widens, it becomes increasingly difficult for him to monitor the results. Incidentally, it's worth remembering that one cannot lay down a numerical limit for a 'maximum' span of effective control, for this will be determined in every case by some daunting, salient factors:

- The personal competence and professional integrity of the manager concerned.

- The overall task and workload of his section or department, and the individual tasks and workloads of his team members.
- The time available to the manager.
- The geographical location of his people.
- And, of course, their individual experience, competence and reliability.

Teaser 3
The 'six-step' process for problem-solving should be engraved on every manager's heart – for it is one of the most vital and, yet, most blatantly ignored aspects of his craft.

1 Identify the problem.
2 Gather all the relevant facts.
3 Establish the cause(s) of the problem.
4 Identify and develop all the possible solutions.
5 Implement the most practical solution.
6 Evaluate the outcome.

And problems with delegation are no exception to this set of eminently practical rules.

Teaser 4
1 Delegate only sufficient authority (which, remember, is power) to enable adequate completion of the task, never more.
2 Allocate sufficient responsibility to make the delegate fairly accountable for success or failure in carrying out the task. And remember who, in the subordinate's view, bears ultimate responsibility – you do!

Teaser 5
1 Ensure that the task concerned is one that should be delegated and is not just being hived off.
2 Ensure that the task is delegated to the member of staff most suited to carry it out.

Teaser 6
Think of any organization or set-up in which the common

herd elects a leadership, to which it then delegates the job of representing it's interests. That's right, one outstanding example is the so-called democratic system of elections and government in this sceptred isle. The process of delegation (however much you may deem it to be wildly out of control) takes place in an upward direction.

6 Run a team, not a prison camp

ACHIEVING THE VITAL TEAM SPIRIT AND FOSTERING IT

Without doubt, one sinister bug which dwells and multiplies in the blood of umpteen managers is the virus of self-deception:

> What do you mean, how do I run my team? Let me tell you, I'm an old hand at the game – why, I've run more teams, as you call them, than you've had hot dinners. Still, if you want to know, I'll tell you – give the blighters an inch, and they'll take a mile. So long as they know who's in control, they'll perform and, make no mistake about it, my lot know. Output – that's all I'm concerned with. If they come up with the goods, okay – but if they don't, I'm on to them in a flash. Got any more silly questions?

> (*A somewhat bellowed comment by an old-school manager at a seminar on 'Leadership' – to which he had been conscripted by a despairing managing director.*)

> Assertive, you say? Well, er, yes – I think I'm, er, assertive . . . aren't I?

> (*What could be construed as a cry for help from one of Nature's shrinking violets at the same seminar.*)

> Good grief, of course, I believe in encouraging a team spirit. Look, all my people know full well that I regard myself as – well, the catalyst. They also know that they can come to me at any time with their problems – after all, that's what I'm here for. (*Knock at the door – it opens to*

reveal one of his subordinates) What in hell . . . get out – can't you see that I'm engaged?

(*A fictional and, we trust, larger than life example.*)

As I've attempted to imply with the above snippets, one rabid manifestation of the ease with which so many managers practise self-deception is their utterly false conviction that they're all-round, good skippers – highly respected leaders of well-knit, happy workteams. In a pig's ear they are.

I think I'll tell you a story to illustrate my point – a true-life tale, suitably tailored to protect the guilty.

THE SAD ACCOUNT OF THE MANAGER WITH MANAGEMENT MYOPIA

Arthur is a late middle-aged and technically gifted design engineer who was lucky enough to achieve a lifetime's ambition by founding his own business. True, it was a very small beginning – quite literally, a hole-in-the-corner engineering outfit where the going was tough, indeed. However, our hero's consistent hard graft paid mounting dividends and, over the years, the firm gradually expanded into what it is today – a smallish company, employing some eighty people, fighting to maintain its niche in an increasingly competitive market. For the record, although it doesn't really matter, we'll say that Grimrod Engineering Ltd designs and produces a range of horizontal, saw-toothed vibrators for the aerospace industry. Of late, and in common with many other firms of similar size and function, GEL has been saddled with unwelcome expenditure arising from the vital necessity to acquire a British Standards Institution 'Kitemark' endorsement for their products, and this hasn't helped their unending struggle to maintain a minimally-healthy bottom line. So, with mounting difficulties on the sales side, a right old upheaval on the production floor and generally strained finances, our scenario backcloth reflects colours of a somewhat dismal hue. But is all this the sum of the company's troubles, or is there more bad news?

You bet your life there is, for we've yet to consider the

subject of our story, GEL's founder – Arthur William Grimrod, Esquire. Here we have a classic example of the senior manager who has clawed himself up the hard way – from engineering apprentice and nightschool student-draughtsman via a rickety, many-runged ladder to the dizzy and, to him, frightening height of MD. As is so often the case, there came the moment in Arthur's life when, many years ago and working for someone else, he was suddenly pitchforked into his first supervisory post – for, in the eyes of his then boss, he was a first-rate worker who stood out as an excellent bet for the job of chargehand. Yes, reader, we're back to the old, old theme. Arthur became a manager by the simple process of being thrown in at the deep end; *sans* training, *sans* development, *sans* everything – except, of course, his enthusiasm, some valuable technical know-how and, as an emergency fall-back, his innate wit and cunning.

And, lest you think otherwise, let me assure you that Arthur was quite successful as a chargehand, not only because he was a responsible and likeable chap who took the job seriously but, also, because he was blessed with workmates who respected him and were therefore quite happy to accept him as their leader. The clincher, if you like, was that he continued to rub shoulders with his ex-mates, treated them fairly and worked enjoyably in their midst.

While everything in Arthur's early management gardens may not have been perfect, there were no major hiccups. Ever keen to learn more of his craft, he attended many technical courses but neither Arthur nor his successive bosses had the foresight to realize that he would derive much benefit from formal and in-depth training in *managing people*. In their defence, it must be admitted that, since he was a fairly astute cookie, Arthur seldom dropped any real clangers – in short, 'things management' got done and, certainly, his various targets were generally achieved. And, remember, so far as his several, like-minded employers were concerned, he was a first-rate design engineer who liked nothing better than to get his hands dirty at the work he loved.

Eventually, there came that momentous day when, financially bolstered by an unexpected legacy from a maiden aunt,

Arthur was able to set up his own business, albeit in a very small way. During the early days of GEL's history (when, as I've already intimated, the going was very difficult) Arthur was once again in his element, working like fury at drawing board and bench – while his wife ran their apology for an office. However, surprise, surprise, as the years went by and the firm expanded, the rot gradually set in and, although he wasn't aware of it at the time, poor old Arthur was to pay the price for his lack of management expertise. This slide into virtual crisis can best be illustrated by cataloguing some of his more costly errors of judgement – so, in the words of the Bard, if you have tears, prepare to shed them now.

All pals together – rankly (and somewhat naturally) paternalistic in his outlook, Arthur had always regarded himself as responsible for the overall well-being of his employees and (again, somewhat naturally) felt that he owed his original small gang an immense debt of gratitude for their unstinted support during GEL's early, hand-to-mouth days. As a consequence, when things improved, he took care to reward this loyalty by carrying his team of old contemptibles along with him and, as the firm expanded, by promoting the best of them to increasingly senior slots. Thus it was that he came to govern what he regarded as a happy band of dedicated brother-managers, all pulling together for the common cause. In cold reality, what he created was a group of so-called executives virtually cloned in his own image; technically able at the start, but inadequately equipped to cope with the unremitting demands of an expanding technology – and hopelessly untutored in the complicated art of management.

Triggered by this state of affairs, it wasn't very long before the original group cohesion started to crack at the seams. Although they have never acknowledged their plight, the fact is that these ill-qualified managers, who are still in the majority at GEL, no longer act as a team but, rather, as a clump of individuals who, frustrated and worried by their many inadequacies, ineffectively paddle their own canoes against a mounting current of difficulties.

The boss commits further self-inflicted injury – plainly, Arthur found it impossible to indulge in across-the-board promotion from within and there were occasions when, faced with this or that management vacancy, he made what he regarded at the time as some very good selection decisions. Talk about self-deception. . . . Take, as a salutary example, the saga of Ron Spence. This ex-engineer had worked for some years as general manager to one of GEL's competitors and, as is so often the case within a small, specialized industry, Arthur had got to know Ron well and had grown to admire him as a person and as a manager. One day, Arthur was saddened to hear out of the blue that Ron had been made redundant and was experiencing great difficulty in landing another job. It so happened that our striving MD heard this news right at the time when he was considering hiring (his words) 'a *real* sales manager' – someone who would supplement his two sales engineers and orchestrate the first actual marketing campaign in GEL's history.

'Aha,' thought Arthur, 'Ron knows the industry better than most – he's been general manager at Green's for years and, as a result, right in the thick of it where aggressive marketing's concerned. He needs a job, he's a rattling good chap and, yes, I need him.' Without further ado, Arthur arranged to meet Ron and, during the course of a very pleasant chat, the fatal deal was struck – Ron became GEL's sales manager.

That was a year ago. Since his appointment, Ron, an autocratically-inclined administrator at heart, has succeeded in alienating all his new and admittedly far less efficient colleagues – but, through sheer lack of experience, has made a complete botch-up of his primary responsibilities as sales manager. Using his dominant personality to the full, he has drawn the wool over Arthur's eyes and convinced the MD that the continuing sales fiasco is entirely due to market conditions and the general unsuitability of GEL's products, anyway. Drawing a hefty salary and limitless expenses, he remains in post and will probably continue making a hash of things until Arthur retires in twelve months' time – if, that is, the firm lasts that long.

There's more than thunderclouds brewing on the shop floor – there can be no better judge of a management's failings than the employees who are forced to endure them, and the GEL workforce is no exception to this grim old rule. Harried from pillar to post by ill-selected and, in the main, poorly qualified supervisors (who, of course, suffer the first-line brunt of their managers' ineptitudes) the people at the grass-roots of the company now flounder in a morass of dissatisfaction and low morale. Consequently and obviously, production tends to stagger on, rather than proceed at a brisk, efficient pace and, among many other things, is constantly beset by very serious problems of quality control. Each such crisis triggers its own management furore, when tempers flare and junior heads are inclined to fall – and, generally speaking, the prognosis looks grim, indeed.

It's at this dismal point that we'll shelve the tale of Arthur and his management myopia – until, that is, you feel sufficiently fortified to tackle this chapter's Workbox, when you'll have an opportunity to poke *your* inquisitive digit into GEL's sorry affairs. In the meantime, let's get on.

SOME THOUGHTS ON CREATING A TEAM

You know, it could be said that we managers are nothing if not optimists. We reap ourselves a bunch of subordinates (either through fateful inheritance or by dint of our own splendid efforts at selection) and, provided we're sufficiently with-it, strive like anything to convert this heterogeneous clump of humanity into what the pundits call a cohesive, effective team. And, yes, optimism or not, come hell or high water, it's an extremely important task.

That being so, we must give this boiling priority more than a passing thought.

For starters, I'd like you to take a brief flight of fancy and imagine that you're standing at the side of the playground at your local infant school, just when the wee mites are coming out to play. Observe what happens and note how, quite haphazardly and for no apparent reason, the children tend to coalesce in clusters – and remind yourself, if reminder is necessary, that what you are witnessing is the magical formation of what the textbooks term natural human groups. Keep looking and it shouldn't be long before you notice that, within the groups, there are those little children who, by dint of sheer personality and/or thumping the others, manage to gain the ascendancy and take over control of their respective bands. Yes, you've got it in one – you're privy to a perfect example of the striving emergence of *natural leaders*.

Cast your eyes around the playground. Do you see that hapless little character over yonder, who's going from group to group with the hope of gaining acceptance and, quick as a flash, is being bounced back out of each and every one? That's right, reader, you've spotted a tearful example of what, in jargonese, we term a *reject*. And, hey, what about that little girl who is sitting on the grass at the side of the playground, intent on making a daisy-chain – all alone, but apparently self-content? Yes, the odds are that you've identified an *isolate*, an individual who, for better or worse, deems it best to remain aloof from the common herd.

Okay, now come back down to earth and consider what happens when people get plonked into the highly artificial work situation. Do all the manifestations of natural behaviour (and I've only mentioned a few) go by the board? Once again, the answer is strikingly obvious – no, they don't. None of the organizational and disciplinary ramifications of the workplace will lessen the sure-fire certainty that, while the imposed official hierarchy may hopefully prevail over the natural human pecking order, it will never supplant it. Thus it is that the cohesion of any work group (and that includes *your* lot) can be endangered by the presence within it of:

1   A burgeoning natural leader who utilizes the power of a dominant personality to undermine the boss's authority and bend other members of the group to his or her will.
2   An employee who, for whatever reason, has been 'rejected' by the group and whose enforced presence is therefore heartily disliked.
3   An isolate-type 'loner', who has no wish to integrate with the group or share in its corporate endeavours.

Having regaled you with that hefty proviso, let's now take a look at the various bricks which, when properly laid, go towards the building of that elusive and intangible thing, team spirit or, as dear old Colonel Blimp would rightly term it, *esprit de corps.*

Common goals

While all the members of the group must be encouraged to achieve their respective and highly individual objectives, it is no less important that the team as a whole is unified by obtaining an across-the-board recognition and acceptance of common goals. But, once again, beware! The autocratic or simply unwise manager who attempts to impose these overall objectives on his people will very soon find himself on a hiding to nothing. Carefully steered discussion is the only true way to win them round – and, just in case you've a dollop of Machiavellian blood running in your veins, this *doesn't* mean acting the part of a con-man.

Team identity

Huh, there are some executive-type creatures who believe that team identity simply means the organizational name of the group – Sludge Inwards Department, or whatever. But you're not one of them, are you? You and I know that this bit of jargon refers to the awareness of a given band of employees that they haven't just been slung together, willy-nilly, but, rather, that they're valued members of a team – people who, knowing each other and each other's capabilities, *belong* together. Yes, it goes without saying, doesn't it – but, and here's the rub, do we also appreciate that the manager is as much a part of the team as the most junior member?

> Oh, my God, here we go again. . . . That's as obvious as the nose on your face, Goodworth – if he's to enjoy any success at all, it stands to reason that the manager's *got* to be part of the team. For heaven's sake, stop teaching me to suck eggs.

All right, smartie-pants – so, tell me, why it is that so many managers address their teams along the following lines?

> Remember the deadline – I want all statements in the post by Friday, at the latest.

instead of

Hey, remember the deadline – we must have all the statements in the post by Friday, at the latest.

or

I'd like you to have a go at. . . .

instead of

I'd like us to have a go at. . . .

or

Joe, Sales have just been on the line. They want that Horrocks order completed this week – do you think it can be done?

instead of

Joe, Sales have just been on the line. They want that Horrocks order completed this week – do you think we can do it?

or

Okay, that's the set-up – so I'd like you to get cracking.

instead of

Okay, that's the set-up – so let's get cracking.

The manager who constantly resorts to the holy pronoun 'I', *et al*, when addressing his people is the boss who remains aloof from them; the kind of leader who'll never, ever be regarded as 'one of us' by the group. Sorry, what was that?

Now you've got me really worried. You're saying that, in order to create a team spirit, a manager should set out to be 'one of the boys' – but I've always understood that that'd be asking for trouble. Surely, a boss has to stay aloof – otherwise, he stands in danger of losing status *and* credibility.

Lest that comment reflects your feeling (which, now that we know each other, would surprise me) it is not only possible but eminently desirable for the truly consultative-cum-participative manager to play the 'one of us' role without losing a shred of status *or* credibility – and play it he should.

Mind you, this business of creating and fostering team identity is not all plain sailing. It's only too easy to overcook things and produce a work group who, because they've come to regard themselves as the bee's knees, compete with other sections and departments in a spirit of destructive rivalry – and, as you'll appreciate, that can be distinctly counter-productive.

Loyalty and cooperation

The with-it manager who succeeds in inculcating his group with team identity and the need to strive for common goals will, in fact, be thrice blessed – for his people will be well on the way to achieving a corporate bond of loyalty and, just as important, a yen for mutual collaboration. In other words, they'll not only think of themselves as a team, they'll *pull together* as a team – and what could be better?

An internal code of behaviour

Quiz any ex-serviceman on this aspect of 'team dynamics' and the odds are that he'll reminisce at length about the manner in which well-knit groups in the forces develop their own, highly unofficial standards and rules of conduct. Provided the leadership is of the right quality (and here we must call to mind the ineptitude of the democratic leader), exactly the same type of phenomena will occur within any group in business or industry; to wit, an internal code of behaviour which, carefully monitored by the thinking boss, will augment, *not* supplant, his authority and do much to improve the efficiency and well-being of the team, as a whole.

TREADING THE DISCIPLINE MINEFIELD – AND SURVIVING

If we're honest, we averagely proficient, run-of-the-mill managers can easily have nightmares over the prospect of wielding the disciplinary whip. Of all the eyeball-to-eyeball confrontations that beset our working lives, there's little doubt that the need to conduct a formal disciplinary interview will set the old butterflies in the tum a'fluttering with renewed vigour – for, to you and I, the prospect of assessing and administering punishment to any employee is nothing if not unpleasant; if only because:

- In dealing with an offender, we are forced to step outside the comforting familiarity of our everyday personality and perform a role which, intrinsically, is foreign to our nature.
- We fear that the event (or, more precisely, our actions) may throw a spanner into the works where our status and/or popularity are concerned.
- We fear that we may drop a procedural clanger of some sort or another.

I'll go further. Any manager who doesn't dislike this hopefully occasional aspect of his duties is suffering from what I'd regard as an unhealthy quirk of personality – and, for what it's worth, I certainly wouldn't like to work under such a creature. So, all in all, I reckon we've got to take more than a passing glance at what an old sage once described to me as the business of being a bastard without acting like one.

Action prior to the dreaded interview

You may think I'm preaching the all-too-obvious, but since an army of managers still succeed in lousing-up their preliminary actions in any disciplinary event (and if you don't believe that, you haven't read many industrial tribunal reports) I make no apology for directing your attention to some basic ground-rules:

1 Whatever the temptation, always refrain from leaping into precipitate action – a calm frame of mind is an essential ingredient of disciplinary success.
2 Ensure that you garner and fully understand all the facts of the case. Unfortunately, this is often easier said than done, particularly in instances of poor performance – but never endanger the process of natural justice by failing to identify, sift and weigh every scrap of relevant information.

3   Examine the facts in the light of your firm's published disciplinary procedure. If, as is so often the case, this is conspicuous by its absence or is skeletal in content, consult the Advisory, Conciliation and Arbitration Services Code of Practice, *Disciplinary Practice and Procedures in Employment*. In other words, ensure that what you have in front of you does, indeed, constitute a disciplinary matter.

The disciplinary interview, itself
Pay strict attention to the following points and, believe me, you won't derail yourself:

1   Adopt a firm and impartial manner. This does not mean that you should leap into an amateurish and wholly false portrayal of the Lord High Justice in swingeing action – unless you're a giggling, immature idiot (which I pray you are not), be yourself.
2   Represent the facts of the case to the employee – fairly and succinctly.
3   Point out the consequences of his action in terms of broken rules or other requirements, loss of production or lowering of personal efficiency, the effects on others, etc.
4   Avoiding subterfuge, try to get the employee to admit that he is in the wrong.
5   Procure the attendance of any witnesses and, by dint of careful probing and questioning, be sure that you understand the facts and weight of their evidence.
6   Do not hesitate to adjourn the session to enable you to consider what has been said – but never prolong such an adjournment unnecessarily. Justice must not only be seen to be done, it must be seen to be done with due expedition.
7   Announce the punishment in clear, unequivocal terms and *never* indulge in a harangue. If the case involves a penalty short of dismissal, provide a degree of hope for the person concerned.
8   Never forget to outline the process of appeal against the punishment.

Some afterthoughts on getting discipline into perspective

I don't know where you keep it, but break off at this point and dig out your much-thumbed dictionary. Look up the word 'discipline' and take careful note of the first definition – which I'll bet you any money goes something like this:

> **discipline** 1 Noun. Training, especially of the kind that produces self-control, orderliness and the capacity for cooperation.

Do you get the point? While, in almost any disciplinary matter, the question of punishment may well occupy our minds, we must never lose sight of the fact that, above all else, discipline is about training and education – improving knowledge, skills, attitudes and performance. And, if you want to be a good disciplinarian, you'll have this reminder engraved on your heart.

As a form of postscript to this little section, I offer an overall objective in disciplinary interviewing for your consideration. If the offender leaves your presence thinking, 'By heck, that was one hell of a rocket, but I deserved it – at least, he was fair' – well, my friend, you've won.

IT'S THE SAME OLD MESSAGE – DISCUSSION BUILDS TEAM SPIRIT

What with one thing and another, the daily grind leaves little apparent time for general discussion with one's team, but, for success, the time must be found. Get them together at regular intervals and make profitable use of the hidden agenda that, if you're wise, you'll always carry in that mental hip pocket:

- *Breaking the ice* – capitalize on a recent success by the team, or any other pleasant topic, to get them talking. If you really have their confidence, an alternative is to regale them with a humorous account of some near-clanger you've recently dropped.
- *Communication* – describe recent developments that, directly or indirectly, will affect the team. Ensure through

discussion, *not* diatribe, that everyone understands all the facts *and* the implications involved.

- *Change* – discuss the immediate and medium-term future of the firm and/or the department in terms of planned or possible developments – covering sales, orders, product-ivity, changes of people, equipment and processes, etc. Remember, once again, that facts are one thing – implic-ations are quite another.

- *Job functions and responsibilities* – seek views on ways and means of improving individual/team efficiency and job satisfaction, removing anomalies, reducing duplication of effort, etc.

- *Training and development* – similarly, seek views on any training or other employee development that, in the opinion of the group as a whole, would be of benefit – task-wise *and* employee-wise.

- *Working conditions* – let this knotty area be a subject for frank and open discussion and, as with all the preceding topics, do not make promises, albeit with the best will in the world, that you cannot keep.

Yes, it's a fact that well-steered and fruitful discussion can be a glorious tonic for the team a a whole. Things only go sour when either the manager fails to come up trumps or, to quote Charles Churchill, because, 'So much they talked, so very little said.' Get cracking, get discussing!

Employee counselling

Some bosses imagine that they discharge their counselling responsibilities by stopping at young Willie's work station every third Friday and mouthing something like, 'Hello, lad –how's it going, then?' But we know better, don't we? Counselling is all about dealing with problems of welfare, attitudes and performance – and it rates as an urgent priority on the manager's interview slop-chit. Some useful points to bear in mind are:

1 Once again, break the ice in a gentle and informal manner. If, however, you are confronted with a welfare problem, don't ruin the whole thing with ghastly attempts at

humour or by telling thoughtless anecdotes. Needless
advice? Oh, no, you'd be amazed what some bosses come
out with on such testing occasions.
2   Steer the interview gently and considerately.
3   Pose open-ended questions, remembering the 'magic six'
– How. . .? Why. . .? What. . .? When. . .? Who. . .?
Where. . .?
4   *Listen* as you've never listened before and give an
occasional sympathetic nod to *show* that you are listening.
5   Watch out for those tell-tale looks in the interviewee's eyes
that so often speak volumes to the astute observer.
6   Take care to summarize progress at intervals.
7   Strive to be objectively impartial – whatever your prejudices (and we all have them) may urge to the contrary.
8   If you are required to pass judgement, always ensure
before doing so that your pontification is reasonable in the
light of *all* the circumstances.

Quality circles

One of the very good ideas to emerge from Japan in recent
years is the concept of quality circles – and, before you mutter
something about the disinclination of your employees to chant
the company anthem, indulge in physical jerks and what-not
before starting work, let me stress that quality circles are very
much your cup of tea.

In essence, they're groups of workers, normally led by their
immediate boss, who get together voluntarily to discuss
problems of quality in production (and, remember, 'production' isn't limited to the shop floor), meeting targets, etc.

Okay, but you've already covered the business of
discussion – why are we going over old ground?

Because, reader, there's a lot more to quality circles than
engaging in discussion. For a kick-off, there's the vital feature
that the group is given training in problem-solving and
analytical techniques – so, if you like, we're talking about a
skilled work process rather than an informal get-together.

The recipe for quality circle success can be summarized as
follows:

1   Once trained, the team (supported by their manager) identifies problems concerned with their work and, taking them one by one, agrees detailed plans for their realistic solution.
2   As the planned activities evolve, the quality circle reviews its progress on a regular basis – highlighting snags and calling on company expertise as and when necessary.
3   When a particular solution has been agreed, the circle presents its findings to management in the form of a detailed analysis of the problem and a step-by-step description of the solution proposed.
4   And here we come to the significant bit – the team, itself, is responsible for putting agreed solutions into effect. It monitors progress and results and reports, accordingly.

I'm sure you'll appreciate the extent to which properly trained and supported quality circles can help tremendously to improve standards of quality and productivity. But that's by no means the end of the story – for quality circles are also the very stuff of which splendid teams are made. True, the initial training will cost a spot of money, but just think of the dividends!

WORKBOX NUMBER 6

Teaser 1
Back to Arthur and Grimrod Engineering Ltd. . . . What follows in Figure 5 is a portion of the firm's management structure, suitably annotated with additional comment. Take a good look at this and, assuming that you are GEL's MD Designate, jot down notes for your future action.

Managing Director
Arthur Grimrod

Due to retire in twelve months' time. No formal training in management – cannot resist frequent forays to design office and production department, where he delights in doing what others regard as meddling. Insists on reading all incoming/outgoing mail before distribution or despatch, stating that this is the only way he can keep his finger on the pulse. A rankly paternalistic manager.

Sales Manager
Ron Spence

Aged 52, ex-general manager with wide admin. experience. No active experience in sales and entirely unsuited to the post. An autocratic and dominating personality who has set out to cloak his weaknesses with quite skilled argument. To be fair, a selection mistake on Grimrod's part. One year's service with firm.

Production Manager
Mike Wallis

Aged 59, ex-engineering fitter, chargehand and production supervisor. Joined firm when first founded in 1964, seven years in present slot. A good organizer, but inclined to show favouritism with shop floor workers. He meets all targets, but is unpopular with design staff, who regard him as someone who is faintly inept when it comes to reading and fully understanding technical drawings and specs. No formal training in man management. Unpopular with a wide section of his workforce.

Projects Engineer John Morris	**Administration Manager Margaret Fletcher**
Aged 53, a versatile and highly experienced designer, well-versed in GEL's industry, who is essentially a 'back-room boy' – popular with his small staff, but not so with his management colleagues, who regard him as something of a criticizing nuisance. There is cogent evidence that JM is stifled and frustrated in his efforts by the MD's constant habit of 'interfering' in the section's activities and projects. Joined firm when first founded in 1964.	Aged 50, ex-accounts clerk and office supervisor. A very good organizer and proficient accountant, experiences some difficulty in relationships with her management colleagues, mainly due to her never-ending struggle to impose very necessary financial stringencies. Dislikes the 'general admin.' aspect of her duties and would much prefer to specialize in finance/accounts, for which work she is highly qualified and suited. Joined firm in 1972.

Figure 5

Teaser 2

Take a look at Figure 6 which summarizes the points made on team-building in this final chapter.

Some suggestions for moulding a team

Examine the group →Identify the natural leaders, rejects and 'loners'

Encourage the members to agree common objectives →By frank and open discussion

Create a firm sense of team identity →By dint of carefully worded communication in all one's dealings with the members

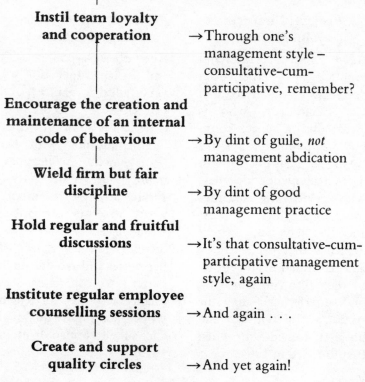

Instil team loyalty and cooperation → Through one's management style – consultative-cum-participative, remember?

Encourage the creation and maintenance of an internal code of behaviour → By dint of guile, *not* management abdication

Wield firm but fair discipline → By dint of good management practice

Hold regular and fruitful discussions → It's that consultative-cum-participative management style, again

Institute regular employee counselling sessions → And again . . .

Create and support quality circles → And yet again!

Figure 6

Using Figure 6 as your keystone, carry out a full and frank audit of the current state of play *vis-à-vis each item* where your work group is concerned.

WORKBOX CRIB BANK

Teaser 1

Perhaps fortunately, I have no way of knowing your precise reaction when you first read this Teaser. So, methinks I'll box on the canny side and, assuming that you were highly annoyed, try to explain my motives in serving up such an open-ended, subjective monster. But, first, I'd like to counter any accusation that the situation depicted at our mythical Grimrod Engineering Ltd is either exaggerated or, for that matter, totally unreal. The sad truth is that the entire story, although presented in ultra-digest form, is based on fact – to the extent that right now, not forty miles from where I sit writing this stuff, a hapless MD Designate is wondering how on earth he's going to deal with an exactly similar situation.

All right, so it's a true story. But I'm not about to take over the reins of any company and, even if I was, the odds that I'd be landed in the same kind of mess are so slim that they can be entirely discounted. And, anyway, you've said it – the thing is so open-ended that I could go on for hours and still not arrive at a decent solution. It's not worth the candle.

I take your point, but bear with me, do. My purpose in posing the Teaser is solely to provide you with a series of triggers for thought – for, as sure as the Great Chairman in the Sky made little apples, there'll come the day (if it hasn't come, already) when you *will* be faced with at least a microsemblance of the GEL saga. The manager who goes through life without coming up bang-smack against an ill-assorted, inefficient number of subordinates at some point in his career is a fortunate man, indeed and, as I've said, I don't rate your chances as really that good. So, let's dispel any feelings of annoyance or frustration and take a gander at the characters portrayed in the GEL organization. I know there are umpteen permutations of thought – we'll just look at some of them.

Ron Spence – Sales Manager
Well, if you've thought about it at all, I'm pretty confident that you've considered Spence as a candidate for the quick bullet. On the surface, he's made a botch-up of his job and, provided, as a fair manager, you go through the business of formal warnings (with specific improvements required within stated periods) you can certainly dismiss him. The devil in you may be inclined to retort, 'Why bother about warnings and all that jazz? The man's only been with the company for a year, he can't complain to a tribunal – I'd just go ahead and kick him out.' Well, that's as may be, but I did assume that you're a fairminded manager.

There is at least one alternative. Albeit that Spence is an autocratic so-and-so, is it not possible that his wide administrative experience can be put to good use elsewhere within the company – particularly in view of Margaret Fletcher's hang-up on the administrative side of her bailiwick? On the evidence available, you may well consider such a course of action to be highly undesirable – but the point is, it must be considered.

Mike Wallis – Production Manager

Doubtless, you've thought of several alternatives where this ageing manager is concerned; for example:

1   Do nothing. This is a definite alternative but, ask yourself, what are the potential snags involved?

2   Dismissal. Well, if you are so minded, this could be a pretty risky alternative and most certainly not the action of a good people-manager. Wallis has had bags of service with the company and, it seems safe to assume, no formal warnings regarding his performance or overall proficiency – in other words, an unfair dismissal case just waiting to happen.

3   Aha, early retirement! All fine and dandy, provided old Wallis agrees.

4   Voluntary redundancy? Yes, but only if you wipe out the post of Production Manager and that seems an unlikely course of action.

5   Oldish soldier he may be, but one *must* consider the prospect of training – for my money, above all the preceding alternatives. He's a long and faithful servant of the company, a good organizer and he meets all his targets – so what about a healthy stab at training in people-management and the necessary technical aspects? I wonder, do you agree or have you gone for some other course of action?

John Morris – Projects Engineer

Is this guy your potential hope of salvation? On the evidence available, it might well be the case that Morris will blossom under your aspiring leadership – so, the very best of luck! Or do you have other ideas?

Margaret Fletcher – Administration Manager

I suggest that this part of your investigation should concentrate on the question of whether or not Fletcher's dislike of 'general admin.' actually merits any action on your part. If you make the assumption (and in this type of exercise you're pretty well bound to make some assumptions) that it would be beneficial to the company and to the lady concerned to remove the yoke of general admin. from her shoulders, that's fine – except, of course, that you'll have to clobber someone else with whatever's entailed, and this could mean creating a new slot.

A second alternative involves the transfer of Spence to the administrative side of the undertaking – and, of course, a third is to merely let Fletcher continue to stew in her mixture of accounts and admin. juice.

All of which brings me to what I regard as the most pressing problem which awaits your expert attention; namely, the all-too-plain disunity of the GEL management (damn it, I nearly added 'team') as a whole. Whatever changes you decide to wreak, short of sacking them all, which is just plain unrealistic in the existing climate, you'll certainly have to send the whole jolly bunch on some in-depth training in attitude-changing and the vitality of teamwork. To get the right quality of training will cost little short of a bomb, but, as I see it, you've got no other choice.

As I intimated earlier, the exercise was intended to provide you with nothing but triggers for thought. I hope it has.

Teaser 2

Now it's my turn to make an assumption. . . . I reckon that if ten people read this book, nine of them won't even bother to attempt this particular exercise, but I'm hoping that you're the glorious exception. In the event that my optimism is misplaced, there's something else to be plonked on record – so here goes. If you think for one moment that merely reading this or any other book will magically convert you into a good people-manager, you really are a prize idiot. *It takes solid, hard work*; work at the sharp end, with and among your subordinates and this exercise constitutes an essential preamble to those labours. The choice is yours, either take refuge in masterly inactivity or get off your butt and do something, right now.

Do you recall the first step in Figure 6 – 'Examine the group'? This doesn't mean just sitting back in your armchair and carrying out a kind of mental browse where your subordinates are concerned. Far from it – what you've got to do is implement *a formal and in-depth survey of each individual*:

1   What are the 'natural behaviour characteristics' of each person?

   ● Does he/she integrate with the group, and to what extent? What is the evidence to support this conclusion?

   ● In what light is he/she regarded by the other members of the group and, again, what is the evidence?

2   If the individual possesses natural leadership tendencies, are these manifested 'for' or 'against' the interests of the group? Remember, here you are concerned with identifying supportive and/or disruptive influences.

3   If you deem an individual to be a reject or 'loner', what is the precise evidence to support such a conclusion?

And, above all, would other managers whom you respect for their people-management expertise, agree with all your conclusions?

I wish you luck with your audit and, more to the point, all good fortune and success in managing your people. 'Bye, now.

RECOMMENDED READING

Bolton, W., *Supervisory Management*, Heinemann, 1986.

Drucker, Peter F., *People and Performance: The Best of Peter Drucker*, Heinemann, 1978.

Goodworth, Clive, *Effective Delegation*, Century Hutchinson, 1985.

Hunt, John, *Managing People at Work*, Pan, 1981.

Terkel, Studs, *Working: People Talk About What They Do All Day and How They Feel About What They Do*, Management Editions (Europe), 1974.

Walsh, John, *The Manager's Problem Solver*, Sphere Reference, 1987.

Additional response columns for Chapter 2

MANAGEMENT QUESTIONNAIRE

Question	Responses	Question	Responses	Question	Responses
1	(. . .) 1	1	(. . .) 1	1	(. . .) 1
	(. . .) 2		(. . .) 2		(. . .) 2
2	(. . .) 3	2	(. . .) 3	2	(. . .) 3
	(. . .) 4		(. . .) 4		(. . .) 4
3	(. . .) 5	3	(. . .) 5	3	(. . .) 5
	(. . .) 6		(. . .) 6		(. . .) 6
	(. . .) 7		(. . .) 7		(. . .) 7
4	(. . .) 8	4	(. . .) 8	4	(. . .) 8
	(. . .) 9		(. . .) 9		(. . .) 9
	(. . .) 10		(. . .) 10		(. . .) 10
5	(. . .) 11	5	(. . .) 11	5	(. . .) 11
	(. . .) 12		(. . .) 12		(. . .) 12
	(. . .) 13		(. . .) 13		(. . .) 13
6	(. . .) 14	6	(. . .) 14	6	(. . .) 14
	(. . .) 15		(. . .) 15		(. . .) 15
7	(. . .) 16	7	(. . .) 16	7	(. . .) 16
	(. . .) 17		(. . .) 17		(. . .) 17
8	(. . .) 18	8	(. . .) 18	8	(. . .) 18
	(. . .) 19		(. . .) 19		(. . .) 19
	(. . .) 20		(. . .) 20		(. . .) 20
9	(. . .) 21	9	(. . .) 21	9	(. . .) 21
	(. . .) 22		(. . .) 22		(. . .) 22
10	(. . .) 23	10	(. . .) 23	10	(. . .) 23
	(. . .) 24		(. . .) 24		(. . .) 24

11	(. . .) 25 (. . .) 26	11	(. . .) 25 (. . .) 26	11	(. . .) 25 (. . .) 26
12	(. . .) 27 (. . .) 28	12	(. . .) 27 (. . .) 28	12	(. . .) 27 (. . .) 28
13	(. . .) 29 (. . .) 30	13	(. . .) 29 (. . .) 30	13	(. . .) 29 (. . .) 30
14	(. . .) 31 (. . .) 32	14	(. . .) 31 (. . .) 32	14	(. . .) 31 (. . .) 32
15	(. . .) 33 (. . .) 34	15	(. . .) 33 (. . .) 34	15	(. . .) 33 (. . .) 34
16	(. . .) 35 (. . .) 36	16	(. . .) 35 (. . .) 36	16	(. . .) 35 (. . .) 36
17	(. . .) 37 (. . .) 38	17	(. . .) 37 (. . .) 38	17	(. . .) 37 (. . .) 38
18	(. . .) 39 (. . .) 40	18	(. . .) 39 (. . .) 40	18	(. . .) 39 (. . .) 40
19	(. . .) 41 (. . .) 42	19	(. . .) 41 (. . .) 42	19	(. . .) 41 (. . .) 42
20	(. . .) 43 (. . .) 44	20	(. . .) 43 (. . .) 44	20	(. . .) 43 (. . .) 44
21	(. . .) 45 (. . .) 46	21	(. . .) 45 (. . .) 46	21	(. . .) 45 (. . .) 46
22	(. . .) 47 (. . .) 48	22	(. . .) 47 (. . .) 48	22	(. . .) 47 (. . .) 48
23	(. . .) 49 (. . .) 50 (. . .) 51	23	(. . .) 49 (. . .) 50 (. . .) 51	23	(. . .) 49 (. . .) 50 (. . .) 51
24	(. . .) 52 (. . .) 53 (. . .) 54	24	(. . .) 52 (. . .) 53 (. . .) 54	24	(. . .) 52 (. . .) 53 (. . .) 54
25	(. . .) 55 (. . .) 56	25	(. . .) 55 (. . .) 56	25	(. . .) 55 (. . .) 56

MANAGEMENT QUESTIONNAIRE – GATHERING THE STRINGS TOGETHER

Question One   7   11   18   23   25   27   30   33
                             35   38   41   44   46   48   49   52

Authoritative scale ««««

| ■ | | | | | | | | | | | | | | | | |

                              2   5   12   15   20   22   24   28
                             36   37   42   43   45   47   50   53

Consultative/participative scale ««««

| ■ | | | | | | | | | | | | | | | | |

Question Two
              3   5   10   15   20   22   26   28   29   31   38   47

Motivation plus scale ««««

| ■ | | | | | | | | | | | | | |

                              1   4   6   14   18   21   25   27   30   32   37   48

Motivation minus scale ««««

| ■ | | | | | | | | | | | | | |

Question Three 5   10   12   16   22   29   33   37   39   56

Security/confidence plus scale ««««

| ■ | | | | | | | | | | |

                              8   11   14   19   21   30   34   38   40   55

Security/confidence minus scale ««««

| ■ | | | | | | | | | | |

Question Four   4   9   13   17   19   27   51   54   55

Apathy/laissez faire scale ««««

| ■ | | | | | | | | | |

Question One   7   11   18   23   25   27   30   33
                             35   38   41   44   46   48   49   52

Authoritative scale ««««

		2	5	12	15	20	22	24	28
		36	37	42	43	45	47	50	53

Consultative/participative scale ««««

Question Two

3	5	10	15	20	22	26	28	29	31	38	47

Motivation plus scale ««««

1	4	6	14	18	21	25	27	30	32	37	48

Motivation minus scale ««««

Question Three 5 10 12 16 22 29 33 37 39 56

Security/confidence plus scale ««««

		8	11	14	19	21	30	34	38	40	55

Security/confidence minus scale ««««

Question Four   4 9 13 17 19 27 51 54 55

Apathy/laissez faire scale ««««

Question One

		7	11	18	23	25	27	30	33
		35	38	41	44	46	48	49	52

Authoritative scale ««««

		2	5	12	15	20	22	24	28
		36	37	42	43	45	47	50	53

Consultative/participative scale ««««

Question Two

3	5	10	15	20	22	26	28	29	31	38	47

Motivation plus scale ‹‹‹‹

▮☐☐☐☐☐☐☐☐☐☐☐

| 1 | 4 | 6 | 14 | 18 | 21 | 25 | 27 | 30 | 32 | 37 | 48 |

Motivation minus scale ‹‹‹‹‹

▮☐☐☐☐☐☐☐☐☐☐☐

Question Three 5 10 12 16 22 29 33 37 39 56

Security/confidence plus scale ‹‹‹‹

▮☐☐☐☐☐☐☐☐☐☐

| 8 | 11 | 14 | 19 | 21 | 30 | 34 | 38 | 40 | 55 |

Security/confidence minus scale ‹‹‹‹

▮☐☐☐☐☐☐☐☐☐☐

Question Four 4 9 13 17 19 27 51 54 55

Apathy/laissez faire scale ‹‹‹‹

▮☐☐☐☐☐☐☐☐☐

A SPOT OF CANDID INTROSPECTION

moody	(. . .)	moody	(. . .)	moody	(. . .)
touchy	(. . .)	touchy	(. . .)	touchy	(. . .)
sociable	(. . .)	sociable	(. . .)	sociable	(. . .)
passive	(. . .)	passive	(. . .)	passive	(. . .)
anxious	(. . .)	anxious	(. . .)	anxious	(. . .)
restless	(. . .)	restless	(. . .)	restless	(. . .)
outgoing	(. . .)	outgoing	(. . .)	outgoing	(. . .)
careful	(. . .)	careful	(. . .)	careful	(. . .)
rigid	(. . .)	rigid	(. . .)	rigid	(. . .)
aggressive	(. . .)	aggressive	(. . .)	aggressive	(. . .)
talkative	(. . .)	talkative	(. . .)	talkative	(. . .)
thoughtful	(. . .)	thoughtful	(. . .)	thoughtful	(. . .)
sober	(. . .)	sober	(. . .)	sober	(. . .)
excitable	(. . .)	excitable	(. . .)	excitable	(. . .)
responsive	(. . .)	responsive	(. . .)	responsive	(. . .)
peaceful	(. . .)	peaceful	(. . .)	peaceful	(. . .)
pessimistic	(. . .)	pessimistic	(. . .)	pessimistic	(. . .)
changeable	(. . .)	changeable	(. . .)	changeable	(. . .)

easygoing	(. . .)	easygoing	(. . .)	easygoing	(. . .)	
controlled	(. . .)	controlled	(. . .)	controlled	(. . .)	
reserved	(. . .)	reserved	(. . .)	reserved	(. . .)	
impulsive	(. . .)	impulsive	(. . .)	impulsive	(. . .)	
lively	(. . .)	lively	(. . .)	lively	(. . .)	
reliable	(. . .)	reliable	(. . .)	reliable	(. . .)	
unsociable	(. . .)	unsociable	(. . .)	unsociable	(. . .)	
optimistic	(. . .)	optimistic	(. . .)	optimistic	(. . .)	
carefree	(. . .)	carefree	(. . .)	carefree	(. . .)	
even-tempered	(. . .)	even-tempered	(. . .)	even-tempered	(. . .)	
quiet	(. . .)	quiet	(. . .)	quiet	(. . .)	
active	(. . .)	active	(. . .)	active	(. . .)	
leaderly	(. . .)	leaderly	(. . .)	leaderly	(. . .)	
calm	(. . .)	calm	(. . .)	calm	(. . .)	

A SPOT OF CANDID INTROSPECTION – POST-MORTEM

Unstable

( ) Moody   Touchy ( )
( ) Anxious   Restless ( )
( ) Rigid   Aggressive ( )
( ) Sober   Excitable ( )
( ) Pessimistic   Changeable ( )
( ) Reserved   Impulsive ( )
( ) Unsociable   Optimistic ( )
( ) Quiet   Active ( )

Introverted   **Extroverted**

( ) Passive   Sociable ( )
( ) Careful   Outgoing ( )
( ) Thoughtful   Talkative ( )
( ) Even-tempered   Responsive ( )
( ) Controlled   Easygoing ( )
( ) Reliable   Leaderly ( )
( ) Peaceful   Carefree ( )
( ) Calm   Lively ( )

Stable

(*Source*: Eysenck H. J., *Fact and Fiction in Psychology*, Penguin, 1965. Reproduced by permission of Penguin Books Ltd)

A SPOT OF CANDID INTROSPECTION – POST-MORTEM

Unstable

( ) Moody	Touchy ( )
( ) Anxious	Restless ( )
( ) Rigid	Aggressive ( )
( ) Sober	Excitable ( )
( ) Pessimistic	Changeable ( )
( ) Reserved	Impulsive ( )
( ) Unsociable	Optimistic ( )
( ) Quiet	Active ( )

Introverted   **Extroverted**

( ) Passive	Sociable ( )
( ) Careful	Outgoing ( )
( ) Thoughtful	Talkative ( )
( ) Even-tempered	Responsive ( )
( ) Controlled	Easygoing ( )
( ) Reliable	Leaderly ( )
( ) Peaceful	Carefree ( )
( ) Calm	Lively ( )

Stable

(*Source*: Eysenck H. J., *Fact and Fiction in Psychology*, Penguin, 1965 Reproduced by permission of Penguin Books Ltd)

A SPOT OF CANDID INTROSPECTION – POST-MORTEM

Unstable

( ) Moody   Touchy ( )
( ) Anxious   Restless ( )
( ) Rigid   Aggressive ( )
( ) Sober   Excitable ( )
( ) Pessimistic   Changeable ( )
( ) Reserved   Impulsive ( )
( ) Unsociable   Optimistic ( )
( ) Quiet   Active ( )

Introverted   **Extroverted**

( ) Passive   Sociable ( )
( ) Careful   Outgoing ( )
( ) Thoughtful   Talkative ( )
( ) Even-tempered   Responsive ( )
( ) Controlled   Easygoing ( )
( ) Reliable   Leaderly ( )
( ) Peaceful   Carefree ( )
( ) Calm   Lively ( )

Stable

(*Source*: Eysenck H. J., *Fact and Fiction in Psychology*, Penguin, 1965. Reproduced by permission of Penguin Books Ltd)

PANIC INDEX

Delegation
    Authority in, 85
    Establishing allocation priorities, 81
    Establishing work priorities, 81
    Making one's requirements known:
        Allocating, 85
        Commanding, 86
        Consulting, 87
        Instructing, 85, 86
        Motivating, 85
        Pleading, 87
        Requesting, 86
    Overdelegation, 89
    Responsibility in, 85
    Reviewing tasks for delegation, 81
    Underdelegation, 88
Discipline
    ACAS Code of Practice, 50, 65
    Action prior to the interview, checklist for, 104
    Disciplinary interview, checklist for the, 105
    Dismissal, test of validity as a punishment, 50
    Getting it into perspective, 106
    Manager's attitudes to, 103
    Policies and procedures, checking validity of, 105
Employee specification
    Explanation of, 63
Functions of management
    Delegation, 80
    'Managing' tasks, 81
    Motivation, 52, 85

'Operating tasks', 81
Hierarchy of human needs, 47
Job analysis, 60
  Explanation of, 60
Job description
  Content of, 61
  Need for, 59
  Typical example of, 62
Job enrichment
  Explanation of, 70
Job evaluation
  Job classification, 66
  Job ranking, 64
  Points rating, 65
Management styles
  Autocratic, 11, 31
  Consultative-participative, 14, 31
  Democratic, 13
  Laissez faire, 12
  Management fraud, 14
  Paternalistic, 13
Manager
  Definition of a, 1
Maslow, Abraham: Hierarchy of human needs
  Ego needs, 48
  Physiological needs, 47
  Safety/security needs, 47
  Self-fulfilment needs, 48
  Social needs, 48
Motivation
  Motivating for results, 52
  Delegation, in, 85
Payment systems
  Objectives of, 72
  List of, 73
Recommended reading, 117
Questionnaires
  A spot of candid introspection, 29
  A spot of candid introspection: response analysis, 34

Knowledge of a subordinate, 41
Knowledge of a subordinate: response analysis, 46
Management questionnaire, 21
Management questionnaire: response analysis, 30
Subordinates
Assassin, recognizing the, 52
Barrack-room lawyer, recognizing the, 52
Counselling, 107
Disciplining, 103
Goebbels-type, recognizing the, 51
Motivating, 52, 85
Poor performers, 49
Requirement to know their private lives, 44
Saboteur, recognizing the, 51
Training of, 67
Suggestion schemes
Discussed, 73
Introducing, checklist for, 74
Team building
Common goals, setting of, 101
Discussion, encouraging and controlling profitable, 106
Employee counselling, 107
Group rejects, identification of, 100
Internal code of behaviour, creating an, 103
Isolates, identification of, 100
Loyalty and cooperation, 103
Natural leaders, identification of, 99
Quality circles, instituting, 108
Team identity, creation of, 101
Training
Evaluation of, 69
Identification of training needs, 67
Open Learning, 69
Planning, 68
Sources, 69
Systematic training, diagram of, 78